Wanted

Wanted

And Other Plays

by

David Epstein

Retriever Press
AN IMPRINT OF RIVERTOWNS BOOKS

Copyright © 2026 by David Epstein. All rights reserved.

No part of this book may be used or reproduced by any means, graphic, electronic, or mechanical, including photocopying, recording, taping, or by any information storage retrieval system without the written permission of the publisher, except in the case of brief quotations embodied in critical articles and reviews.

This book is human authored.

NO AI TRAINING: Without in any way limiting the author's and publisher's exclusive rights under copyright, any use of this publication to train generative artificial intelligence (AI) technologies to generate text is expressly prohibited. The author reserves all rights to license uses of this work for generative AI training and development of machine learning language models.

"They Told Me That You Came This Way" was originally published in *yale/theatre*, vol. 2, no. 2, pp. 31-39. Copyright 1969, David Epstein. All rights reserved.

Paperback edition ISBN-13: 978-1-953943-78-1
Electronic edition ISBN-13: 978-1-953943-79-8

LCCN Imprint Name: Retriever Press
Library of Congress Control Number: 2026935866

Retriever Press is an imprint of Rivertowns Books. Copies of this book are available from all bookstores, other stores that carry books, and online retailers. Requests for information and other correspondence may be addressed to:

> Retriever Press
> 240 Locust Lane
> Irvington NY 10533
> Info@rivertownsbooks.com

For My Father

Contents

Preface	7
Wanted	9
They Told Me You Came This Way	145
Mine	173
Deceived by Colin Powell	213
Acknowledgments	323
About the Author	324

Preface

THESE PLAYS span a lifetime.

To wrestle with the dramatic form for decades has been an exhilarating, infuriating, nonstop challenge. Love it or run for the hills.

The passion, humor, and ideas that come through any play reflect those days during which it was written and are an expression of who the writer was and was becoming. Choosing these plays, re-entering each world, meeting up with characters I once lived with has been confirming and invigorating.

Playwrights have forever been intrigued by how humans react under pressure. The plays in this volume spark around crises internal and external—situations forcing people to confront and uncover themselves. And, as conflicts and complications evolve on stage character is revealed, questions raised and I fervently hope, audiences are entertained and challenged. We need both now more than ever.

Autumn 2025
Dune Alpin Farm

WANTED

A Play by
David Epstein

Music and Lyrics by
Al Carmines

WANTED

opened at The Judson Poet's Theatre in the fall of 1970. It was directed by Lawrence Kornfeld with the following cast:

Jacob Hooper	Merwyn Goldsmith
Jesse James	Jerry Whelan
Billy The Kid	Jeff Jonaway
John Dillinger	Frank Coppola
Ma Barker	Lee Guilliatt
Opal	Cecilia Cooper
Babycakes	Jerry Clark
Starr Faithful Brown	Andra Akers
Shorty	June Gable
Deafy	Gordon Minard
Old Timer	Stuart Silver
Miss Suzannah Figgit	Gretchen Van Aken
Alistine	Joanne Kyd
Jailer	Gordon Minard
Doc Barker	Stuart Silver
Jelly Barker	John Kuhner
Chief Flaherty	Gordon Minard

WANTED

moved Off-Broadway to the Cherry Lane Theater in the spring of 1971. It was directed by Lawrence Kornfeld with the following cast:

Star Faithful Brown	Andra Akers
Billy The Kid	Reathel Bean
Babycakes	Jerry Clark
Opal	Cecilia Cooper
John Dillinger	Frank Coppola
Shorty	June Gable
Jacob Hooper	Merwyn Goldsmith
Ma Barker.	Lee Guilliatt
Deafy	John Kuhner
Jesse James	Peter Lombard
Sheriff Sweet	Stuart Silver
Miss Suzannah Figgit	Gretchen Van Aken
Doc Barker	Stuart Silver
Jelly Barker	John Kuhner
Sister Pohatan Lace	Gretchen Van Aken

ACT ONE

Scene 1

JACOB HOOPER appears in a spotlight, VOICES SING his name. Light fades on Hooper.

JESSE JAMES steps out followed by BILLY THE KID, JOHN DILLINGER, MA BARKER.

JESSE
Wanted: Jesse James the outlaw, for preaching, organizing and demonstrating against the Indian War, for murder, and reckless pacifism.

BILLY
Wanted: William Bonney, alias Billy The Kid, for aiding and abetting the Indian enemy and for murder in every degree.

JOHNNIE
Wanted: John Dillinger, for fund raising for the Indian treasury, for murder and libelous remarks.

MA
Wanted: Arizona Kate Clark, alias Ma Barker, for conspiring to comfort the Indian, for murder, and for procreating with an eye towards grand larceny.

Intro music, Billy, Jesse, Johnnie, and Ma spotlighted.

                   ALL
Wanted: Jacob Hooper...

                 JOHNNIE
... For violent verbosity.

                   ALL
Wanted: Jacob Hooper...

                  BILLY
... For vulgar self-indulgence.

                   ALL
Wanted: Jacob Hooper...

                  JESSE
... For volatile ignorance.

                   ALL
Wanted: Jacob Hooper...

                    MA
... For vicious patriotism.

                   ALL
Wanted: Jacob Hooper, for crimes and crimes and crimes!

Scene 2

Jacob Hooper wears a small American flag on his belt. OPAL, a toughie, and BABYCAKES, an ephebe, stand on either side of him as he speaks out, delivering an address to trainees.

HOOPER
Good morning, investigator-trainees.

This is an aboriginal riddle. It concerns our enemy, our foe. Please take out your riddle notebooks, and a number two pencil.

You are in a desert between two high dunes.

You are disguised as a helpless girl. As the sun drops a lone man approaches on a foaming horse. A pinto. He stops ten yards away. The horse dies. He dismounts. He wears a loin cloth. His skin is reddish, his hair is dark and straight and long. There is a feather in it. He lights a huge fire.

He takes a knife from his belt, makes an incision just below his throat down to his belly button. He reaches in and removes his heart, warms it over a fire and eats it slowly. You are hungry, too.

Then he steps into the fire, smiling, sits down cross-legged and begins to hum. You are moved: the twilight, the desert, the fire, the humming. All the sand you need to put out the blaze and save his life is at your feet.
(long pause)
Now, can you trust this man?

(turns to his agents)

Well?

OPAL

Tough.

BABYCAKES

Mr. Hooper, it was an analogy of such cleverly disguised suspicion that only the most lucidly endowed applicants will be capable of deciphering its verisimilitude.

HOOPER
(a beat)

You know, if I ever felt the two of you were deceiving me, I could—

OPAL

Jacob!

BABYCAKES

Mr. Hooper!

HOOPER

Just a warning. Wash your hands twice. Let's get to work.

OPAL

What's on the agenda, Jacob?

HOOPER

On the agenda:
Nine to eleven—invidious investigation.

Eleven to one—insidious instigation.
One to one-thirty—public relations.
One-thirty to two—recess.
Two to three—gas and germs.
Three to four—man hunt.
Four to four-thirty—witch hunt.
Four-thirty-to five—prayer and solitude.

> *(to himself)*

I'll pray for a lady friend, a parasol lady!

Any word from Alistine, Captain Pussy Posse?

OPAL

Not yet, Jacob. Alistine is in disguise, looking for Ma Barker. She'll check in.

HOOPER

Help me out.

> *They assist him offstage. His right hand automatically fondles Babycakes.*

Scene 3

Jesse James appears, a gaunt man in a hard light.

JESSE

I am the man that hath seen affliction.

There is a war on this land. Indians are dying. Their flesh is the meat and their blood is the gravy of our "leaders." Their bones will be the history of us all.
(pause)
I am gathering strong men and brave women to band against this war. We will resist all the—
(troubled)
I get visions! I see the end. I see us all hanging loose and broken, all of us swinging side by side—twisted broken chicken-necks.
(pause)
They expect me to stay peaceful while they butcher people left and right! I will do whatever the lord sees fit until this killing and this horror have passed.

Jess exits. Billy enters, singing.

SONG: "I'M ON THE RUN"

BILLY

I'm on the run
always on the run
I'm on the run
'cause I'm known.
They got my picture

on every lonesome tree
Wanted: Billy The Kid,
that's me.

It's a funny feeling
running from yourself.
Every time I see my picture
I know I've got to scat
get out on the prairie
where there's nothing but the hoot owls
prairie dogs and that
I'm on the run
'cause I'm known.

And when the moon rises over the prairie
I get so lonesome
I could puke.
Sometimes you get enough of pretty scenery
sometimes you don't care about the view.
Can't you see I'm on the run
with my horse, my pack and my gun
running from my picture
running from the law
running from the daylight
running from my paw and my maw
and the moon and the sun
I'm on the run,
God—it's fun!

I'm on the run
with my spin riding light

under the moon so quiet.
You can hear a stone underfoot
but I shoot and I ride
with a certain amount of pride
'cause I'm different from everything else I see.
I'm famous—I'm wanted—I'm—oh Jesus
when the moon rises over the prairie
I get so lonesome I could shit.
What's the use of being a Known
when you can't enjoy it?

I'm on the run
I'm always on the move
moving too fast for long-time feelings
like friendship and love
it's the price you play for doing what you please
it's the price you always pay for being free.
I ain't sorry—this is how it had to be.
After all, my picture's up on every fence post, every tree
Wanted—Billy the Kid—that's me—that's me!

SONG ENDS

See this town? Called Gulch. Nothin' fancy to look at, but she's a hummer! I come in here last winter for a spell, turned into a stay. Sheriff of this town's a sweet. I just paid a visit—so I'll be okay here for a spell. Times you hit a town an' they telegraph for Jacob Hooper, can't rest a night. So I make a deal, find a town like Gulch with a sweet sheriff—it's better'n nothin'—don't last that long. If you need the warm bad, then it's worth it.

Noon. My Uncle Jeb always said, "Noon's when there's no shadows." I been lookin' all over for Uncle Jeb. He had a lotta sayin's. I tried workin' up some but I couldn't get the hang. I'm uneducated—I ain't dumb! I just haven't had the time. Know why they're after me? I thought this thing out. Cause I'm agin' the way they're killin' Injuns like Jesse is? Or prob'ly cause I got no regular job. They'll hunt you and kill you, masked men.

Last time I was here, I made a friend named Stash. He got shot up the nose, that's a bad place. Nobody wants to get shot up the nose. Old Stash he was a good guy—smelled like cow plop but you shouldda heard him sing! Nobody wants to get shot up the nose.
(whirls and spins around)
That's my spin! I got the wheelinest spin in the whole damn west! Spin'll save your life.

A pretty girl walks by.

BILLY

Hi there, Miss!

STARR FAITHFUL

Hi, yourself!

BILLY

You must be new in Gulch. You from St. Louis?

STARR FAITHFUL

Yep. What's your name?

BILLY

Billy.

STARR FAITHFUL

Billy what?

BILLY

The Kid. What's yours?

STARR FAITHFUL

Starr Faithful Brown. What are you thinking about?

BILLY

Sunsets and dyin' young.

> *He wheels, spins, draws his gun. She pulls a knife and flings it skillfully. We hear a groan from offstage. They exchange smiles.*

Where's you learn that?

STARR FAITHFUL

Finishing school.

BILLY

Can you ride like a man?

STARR FAITHFUL

Stirrups and spurs.

BILLY
Bareback or saddle?

STARR FAITHFUL
Saddle.

BILLY
English or western?

STARR FAITHFUL
American goddamit! And I give a great blowjob.

BILLY
Stirrups or spurs?

STARR FAITHFUL
Spurs.

BILLY
Bareback or saddle?

STARR FAITHFUL
Bareback.

BILLY
English or western?

STARR FAITHFUL
American goddamit!

SONG: "WHERE HAVE YOU BEEN"

BILLY

Where have you been up to now, girl
You could've saved me a lifetime of grief
I didn't know there was one around like you, girl
Alone forever was my motto, my belief.

STARR FAITHFUL

My belief was just like yours, Billy boy
I thought I'd spend my life alone somehow
And I told myself I didn't really mind it
But where have you been up to now?

BILLY & STARR FAITHFUL

Where have you been up to now?
Why weren't you around when I needed you?
I've lived my whole life asking why and asking how
Where have you been up to now?

BILLY

I've fucked around and sucked around this country
There's not a piece of ass that I don't know
I thought something new would never happen
My fucking sucking way alone I'd go.

STARR FAITHFUL

Some guy'd ask me out and I'd go with him
His hands were hot as fire but his eyes were blank as lead
The first time I felt looked at was when you looked at me
Your eyes nudged me into life

Theirs all made me feel dead.

BILLY
You're like the smell of bacon frying when I'm hungry.

STARR FAITHFUL
You're like a piece of velvet I've just got to touch.

BILLY
You're like a song when up to now I've just heard screech owls, Starr Faithful

STARR FAITHFUL
Billy boy

BILLY & STARR FAITHFUL
I love you so much!
Where have you been up to now?
Why weren't you around when I needed you?
I've lived my whole life asking why and asking how
Where have you been up to now?

SONG ENDS

Scene 4

JOHN DILLINGER writes a letter home. DEAFY his accomplice and SHORTY his girl are putting bombs together.

JOHNNIE

"Dear Sis, I thought I would write you a few lines and let you know I am still perculatin'. Don't worry about me, honey, for that won't help any. I am sending Emmett my toy gun and I want him to always keep it. I see that Deputy Blunk says I had a real forty-five, that's just a lot of hooey to cover up because they won't admit that I locked up eight deputies and a dozen trustees with a toy gun. You shouldda seen the look on their faces. Ha! Ha! Ha! Pulling that off was worth ten years of my life. Ha! Ha! Don't part with my toy gun for any price. For when you feel blue all you'll have to do is look at the gun and laugh your blues away. Now Sis, if any of you need anything just let me know. I got shot a week ago but I'm Okay now, just a little sore. Well, I guess I'll close for now. Give my regards to all. Lots of love from Johnnie." That oughtta hold the bastards for a while.

Deafy, pass the nitro. Deafy!

DEAFY
(checks his watch)
Noon, Johnnie. Noon's when there's no shadows.

JOHNNIE
Pass the stuff.

                    DEAFY

Here ya go, Johnnie. Now don't shake it or we'll go sky high. Know what I'm tryin' to bring out here?

                    JOHNNIE

Right.

                    DEAFY

What?

                    JOHNNIE

Right!

                    DEAFY

Okay, then.

                    JOHNNIE

Shorty?

                    SHORTY

Yes, Johnnie?

                    JOHNNIE

Are you happy?

                    SHORTY

Very happy, Johnnie. We'll blow that bank sky-high.

                    JOHNNIE

You don't have to talk like the rest of us around here, you know.

SHORTY

I know, but I'm not playing a game, Johnnie. I'm here for keeps, honest. Come on, let's get these finished.

JOHNNIE

Tell me again.

SHORTY

Banks are the basic foundation of the capitalist system upon which the entire economic superstructure of the war against the Indians rests. Destroy the foundation, totter the superstructure, crumble the system.

JOHNNIE

End the war but get out with the dough-re-me!

SHORTY

Who's to blame?

JOHNNIE

The rich. Who's to save?

SHORTY

The Indians!

JOHNNIE & SHORTY

What's to abolish? The system!

                    DEAFY

Okay, okay, don't have to yell. I can hear you fer chrissake, you'll blow the whole place sky-high. Sensitive to sound, you know what I'm tryin' to bring out here?

            Johnnie and Shorty laugh.

                    DEAFY

Okay, then.

Scene 5

Billy enters looking around. He spots someone offstage.

BILLY

Hi there, you Miss Suzannah?

VOICE

I'm Mabel. Come on inside!

He recoils. A WOMAN enters.

BILLY

Miss Suzannah?

MISS SUZANNAH

Yep.

BILLY

I'm Billy, Starr Faithful's friend.

MISS SUZANNAH

Whose what?

BILLY

Starr Faithful Brown, from back east. Your niece?

MISS SUZANNAH

Oh, my niece, nice girl. Too much culture but a real nice girl. You're very well put together, young man.

                    BILLY

Thank you, mam.

                    MISS SUZANNAH

Sweat a lot do you, hmm?

                    BILLY

Sweat? Well, I reckon—

                    MISS SUZANNAH

Hot sweat pours off ya, ripples down your spine like a river in the desert. Beads of sweat runnin' all over them tight muscles while you're out in the scorchland gettin' stronger and tan thinkin' about women. Think about women much, do you, sonny?

                    BILLY

Yes, mam. I—

                    MISS SUZANNAH

Don't mind Mabel, there. Sometimes I think she pleasures herself with a cactus pear. That's not funny. Get one of them softies, soft in the middle? You'll get a surprise—snap right off on ya. Quite a problem there. You superstitious? She got warts all over her right hand. Whatta you make of that? State your business.

            He's about to answer when Starr Faithful enters running.

                    STARR FAITHFUL

Billy!

                    BILLY
Starr Faithful!

Big hug.

                MISS SUZANNAH
Friend of yours?

                STARR FAITHFUL
Aunt Suzannah, it gives me great pleasure to introduce you to Billy The Kid. Billy it gives me great pleasure to introduce you to my Aunt Suzannah Figgit.

                MISS SUZANNAH
May we rest in peace. Why I sent you back east, I'll never know, 'cept it was in your mother's will.

                STARR FAITHFUL
Mother and my little brother Randolph were captured by the Indians.

                MISS SUZANNAH
Run off with a redskin's what she done.

Starr Faithful gasps in surprise.

Well, it's high time you heard the truth. She always had a thing for injuns. He was a chief—dark coppery skin, lean and tight, built like a horsewhip. She loved him.

BILLY

What was he called?

MISS SUZANNAH

Chief.

STARR FAITHFUL

How do we know mama's dead?

MISS SUZANNAH

We don't.

STARR FAITHFUL

And I wasted all that time back east, just because it was in her will? She might be alive today, we could find her!

MISS SUZANNAH

Maybe she don't wanna be found.

STARR FAITHFUL

Come on Billy, let's go!

BILLY

Go?

MISS SUZANNAH

Hold on, niece. This young man's been suckin' dust for months. Take a look at him, take a close look. Smell him, smell him close—you're smellin' man, niece, man. And less I miss my guess he's after a bed, with sheets!

BILLY
It's the truth.

MISS SUZANNAH
(to Starr Faithful)
Don't pout. Nobody pouts in Gulch. Pout in St. Louis. Pout in Joplin but don't pout in Gulch.
(to Billy)
Now I can give you room with a bed, a room with a bed and a bath, a room with a bed, no bath and flies, or my room, and bed. Big bath.

STARR FAITHFUL
(grabs his hand)
We're going to my room.

BILLY
(as she pulls him offstage)
Much obliged, Aunt Suzannah!

MISS SUZANNAH
You sure are. Now don't you two go doin' any sex things up there behind my back—call me!

SONG: "OUTLAW MAN"

They call me Miss Suzannah Figgit
I'm Miss Figgit—can you dig it?
I'm the horny goddess of the Golden West
I like a man who's tan and lean
A man who's slightly mean

An outlaw is what I like the best.

Yes, a gun will always win me
When everything else fails
I get within a mile of one
And start to bite my nails
I love an outlaw man
It gives me such a thrill
To see his gun all hot and smoky
And I guess it always will
Outlaw man, you're the one for me.
I'd rather be your prisoner
Than live without you and be free.

When I see that holster bulging
I just go into a spin
I can feel that shiny steel
Against my soft white skin
Outlaw man, let me feel your gun
Outlaw man, you're my only one
I'll take it from the holster
Fondle and caress it
I know that it's perversion
But I might as well confess it
Outlaw man, you're my only one.

Outlaw man, let me touch your gun
I promise I won't keep it
'Cause I see you're getting eager
I'll give it right back to you
When you're ready to pull the trigger

Outlaw man, give it to me
Or I'll never let you rest
'Cause I'm Miss Suzannah Figgit—can you dig it?
The horny goddess of the Golden West
The horny goddess of the Golden West.

SONG ENDS

Scene 6

Opal carries a dummy out on a chair. Jacob Hooper stands behind it. He motions Opal to move aside.

HOOPER

Gentlemen, a demonstration, pay attention, do not take notes. If this man has never been found guilty of a crime, any crime, if he has never spent a moment behind bars, if he has never been or said to be the acquaintance of a criminal or a suspected criminal, if he has never admitted anything or been accused of anything, then he is frequently entitled to the rights of a normal citizen. And don't you forget it.

(pause)

No man is guilty until proven guilty—or highly highly suspect. One more thing: personal vendettas and the law don't mix. If you've got a private reason to hate somebody's guts—take care of it on your own time. These tactics . . .

He puts a glove on, pokes the dummy violently in the chest and face, removes its fingernails with a pliers, slaps his head repeatedly—getting into it so much that Opal has to tap him on the shoulder. He stops, breathing heavily.

. . . are not our tactics. If any agent ever treats a totally innocent man in this manner he will answer to me personally. I tolerate no deviance. We already know each and every one of you very very well. Dismissed.

Opal carries the dummy offstage. Hooper moves downstage where a light comes up on Babycakes.

Babycakes, any messages?

BABYCAKES

While you were out: your mother called at one-fifteen.

HOOPER

Well?

BABYCAKES
(pulls out notepad)

No message.
(Hooper nods)
While you were out: a stranger in a long, black coat, white gloves, a carnation, and no hat stopped by.
(checks notepad)
No message.
(Hooper nods)
While you were out: your mother called at one-eighteen.

HOOPER

No message?

BABYCAKES

A note: "Jacob darling, no message."

HOOPER

Where is everybody?

BABYCAKES

The war room. Oh, Mr. Hooper, you did get one message. It just came in from Gulch, Sheriff Sweet.

HOOPER
(smiles)
Oh? What did Sweet have to say?

BABYCAKES
"Dot dot dot, dash dot dash, dash dash dash, dot dot dot—dash!"

HOOPER
Trouble.

BABYCAKES
There's more: "Dash dot dash dot dash dot. Dot dot dot, Dash dash dash. Dash dash." More trouble?

HOOPER
(a little smile)
No message.

Something vile is afoot in the land. I can hear it. I can smell it. I can feel it. It sounds like the nasty whisper of traitors. It smells like the rancid sweat of cowards. It feel like ashes at the foot of a stake.

Find Captain Pussy Posse!

OPAL
Where is she, Jacob?

HOOPER
How'm I supposed to know? She's on her own, eavesdropping, spying, infiltrating. She's—

ALISTINE Enters, dazed.

ALISTINE

She's right here.

HOOPER

Alistine, where have you been?

ALISTINE

I've been had, Mr. Hooper. Something tells me I'm too young to be an undercover girl, or too curious, or too generous, or too warm, or too giving, or too—

HOOPER

Ridiculous! You're tough as nails, just like the rest of us.

ALISTINE

I question that, Mr. Hooper. I've been in love fourteen times in six days and I've gathered no valuable information. In fact, I'm afraid I've given some away. I feel I should resign my commission!

HOOPER

The Captain of the Pussy Posse deals in broken hearts, I told you that when I forced you to take the job. Now don't upset me! Isn't it enough I have the underworld on my back without worrying about you?
(takes a deep breath)
Now, time for morning devotions. Opal, Babycakes! Opal will lead the meditation this morning.

OPAL

The hymn is "Men Roam The Country."

ALL

Men roam the country
Villains out for evil
To pervert the American way
We won't rest in peace
'Till we see them in their graves. Amen.

OPAL

Let us repeat our pledge: Why did they go astray?

BABYCAKES

They disagreed with their elders.

HOOPER

They refused to earn a daily wage.

ALISTINE

When they didn't get their way, they would speak up.

ALL

Shame on them. Shame on them.

OPAL

The sermonette is entitled: "Who's On Our Side."

SONG: "WHO'S ON OUR SIDE"

                    ALL

We've got deadly devices
Every gadget that the law allows:

1. Stool pigeons
2. Canaries
3. Judges
4. Cops
5. Witnesses with perfect memories
6. Witnesses with honest lies.

Shame on them!

SONG ENDS

                    OPAL

Mr. Hooper, will you pronounce the benediction?

                    HOOPER

They shall be caught.

                    ALL

They shall be caught.

                    HOOPER

Jacob Hooper is the law.

                    ALL

Jacob Hooper is the law.

HOOPER

I am the law. I am the law. I am the law.

ALL

Amen.

HOOPER

Opal, that was a very moving sermon. Now I want you to go down to Gulch—
(stops short)
I'm getting an idea. I've got an idea! Round them all up in one place at one time!

BABYCAKES

A party?

HOOPER

A party? An affair! A distinguished affair for riffraff. Maybe a—a ball. A Benefit Ball—for the Indians! Spread a rumor: an Indian Benefit Ball! Use our private mailing list—an anonymous invitation to every name in the business, a chance to get together. They'll snap at it!
(to Alistine)
I want you to infiltrate. Disguise yourself as Edna "Rabbits" Volney, the notorious escape artist.

She salutes, exits.

HOOPER
(to Babycakes)
Get going on that rumor.

Babycakes exits.

I've got work to do: an Indian Benefit Ball. We're going to Gulch. Oh, maybe I'll meet my parasol lady in Gulch!

SONG: "PARASOL LADY"

                             HOOPER

My parasol lady
Where can she be?
The parasol lady
Just for me
She'll be dainty as sugar,
Perky as spice, everything nice
My parasol lady will be
You'll see!

Sometimes in the midst of my profession
I dream that I'm a flesh and blood
Human being like other men
I come home from work
She's waiting with a smile.
She's petite
She's sweet
Always neat
(Not a lousy slob like my mother for God's sake).
Where can she be?
My parasol lady
Just for me.

Sometimes I'm chasing Mugsy or Bugsy or Jesse or John

But hovering above me
Is someone who'll love me
Who's leading me on.
When we meet, she'll say, "Oh Mr. Hooper,
I've heard of you so much so much!
You're so brave and courageous
Distinguished and patriotic and such and such!"
She'll place her tiny hand in mind
I'll embrace her and kiss her
But I'll be gentle and refined
(Not like my mother's sloppy wet kisses for God's sake).
My parasol lady
Where can she be?
The parasol lady
Just for me.

She'll come to me some day, somehow, you'll see,
And when I meet her, there'll be
Blue skies
Clean living
Nothing will make us fall
Off we'll waltz together, forever,
Under her dainty lacy parasol
(Not like my mother's dirty old black umbrella for God's sake).
Parasol lady, wherever you may be
Wait for me!

SONG ENDS

Scene 7

Ma Barker is alone in jail.

MA

Cocksuckers! My boys'll get me the hell outta here before sunup. You hear me? I'm Ma Barker, Ma Barker!
(softly)
Anybody hear me? I'm not just some nobody off the street. You don't know who you're dealin' with.

I could get lost in here, this is no two-bit tank. This is The Cut. No poetry to read. Who's to keep me company? I've heard what happens to women in The Cut. They break your heart, if they don't turn it to stone first. They forget about you. A woman could age fast, nobody to look after her, no spouse or nothin'—always thinkin' back to that first little family she lost—
(summoning courage)
I'm Ma Barker! And my Doc and Jelly'll show before long. They'll show!

Scene 8

Outside The Cut. Doc, Jelly, and RABBITS (Alistine) move quickly.

DOC
Wait'll we tell Ma—Rabbits Volney! One of her true heroes—imagine meetin' Rabbits outside our own front door! Why, she's busted outta more lockups than any man alive.

RABBITS
True heroes—

JELLY
Ma'll be so proud of me! Just bumpin' into her outta thin air like that.

RABBITS
Thin air—

DOC
Proud of you? She bumped into me.

JELLY
(suspiciously)
I thought I wuz alone?

DOC
How could she bump into you if you wuz alone, Jelly? Come on. Rabbits says she'd be down along here somewheres—

MA
(whispers)

Boys!

DOC

Ma! It's Ma, Jelly.

JELLY

Hi Ma!

DOC

Hey, yer lookin' swell, Ma.

JELLY

How's it been goin'? Whatcha been doin'? We missed ya, Ma!

MA

Quit the stupidity and get me the hell outta here.

Doc and Jelly proudly step aside and let Rabbits approach the bars. She lifts one side of them and Ma, astonished, steps out.

MA

Who's this?

DOC & JELLY

Rabbits Volney.

MA

Rabbits Volney! But—you're so short. You used to be tall.

> RABBITS
> *(sadly)*

I used to be.

> MA

Oh, I'm sorry honey. I know how it is. I had an uncle kept gettin' shorter and shorter, too.

> JELLY

Come on, Ma, let's git!

> *They exit quickly.*

Scene 9

Billy and Starr Faithful are in bed.

STARR FAITHFUL
What's wrong, Billy?

BILLY
Nothin'.

STARR FAITHFUL
Billy—

BILLY
I had a haunty dream. Somethin' don't feel right.

STARR FAITHFUL
Why don't you take off your guns?

BILLY
Jesse's right, we gotta keep movin', movin', and talkin'. I ain't done nothin' for the Indians since I got here.

STARR FAITHFUL
What was the haunty dream about?

BILLY
Gettin' shot fat an sloppy in bed. I'd die of shame if I ever got kilt in a bed.

STARR FAITHFUL

For a guy who camps on the range you do just fine in a bed.

BILLY

How do you mean?

STARR FAITHFUL

You've got the fastest spin in the west.

BILLY

I'm gonna have to scoot.

STARR FAITHFUL

I'm going too! You taught me ride, you taught me to shoot and you owe it to me, I saved your life the day I met you.

BILLY

Nope. You got no idea what it's like bein' hunted, runnin' from things you never done cause you might once've done somethin'. Chased all over your own country. There's no gettin' out.

STARR FAITHFUL

Who says? Why not? Why can't you change?

BILLY

You can't. Can't go changin' who you been. They won't let you. They'd rather have 'em a bad hero keeps havin' to kill people to stay alive than have no hero at all, livin' on a farm.

STARR FAITHFUL

Well, I know what it's like not being hunted and I'm tired of it. We'll do something constructive. We'll locate Mama and my brother Randolph.

BILLY

Nope. Listen. I'm gonna get kllt. It's my fact—everybody's got a fact, some people know 'em soon, some people never know 'em. Gettin' kilt is mine. Anybody rides with me gets kilt, too.

STARR FAITHFUL

That sounds better than dying.

BILLY

Don't argue with me, Starr Faithful.

STARR FAITHFUL

Why shouldn't I?

BILLY

'Cause I'm the man, dammit!

STARR FAITHFUL

So what? If you fall in love with somebody who loves you back then you don't just ride out on them the way you rode in.

BILLY

I can do whatever I want, Starr Faithful.

STARR FAITHFUL
(pause)
So can I, Billy. And I'm riding with you!

SONG: "I WANT TO RIDE WITH YOU" (lyrics by David Epstein)

Have you been waiting every noon
in the middle of some town
for someone just to stop and say I love you?
A stranger tall and long who sings a private song
and the burden of his song is just I love you.

I want to ride with you
through the shadow of your trails
I want to ride with you
into the ivory sunshine of your smile.

BILLY
I don't know how long the ride will last,
some rides are over mighty fast.

STARR FAITHFUL
I don't care as long as I can ride with you
one morning on the trail with you
would make my life worth living through.
I'd do it even if I knew it wouldn't last.
If I didn't have a future, at least I'd have a past.

BILLY & STARR FAITHFUL
I want to ride with you
through the shadow of your trails

I want to ride with you
into the ivory sunshine of your smile.

If we could share every sunset
be at peace with every noon
open every morning with your eyes
every morning of our lives . . .
I want to ride with you
 I want to ride with you.

BILLY

Who cares how long we have together?
It's long enough as long as we're together
and I can hear you laugh and watch you sleep forever
if forever's just a day . . .
I've waited a lifetime just to live today.

BILLY & STARR FAITHFUL

I want to ride with you
through the shadow of your trails
I want to ride with you
into the ivory sunshine of your smile.

SONG ENDS

Miss Suzannah walks in.

MISS SUZANNAH

Billy, Sheriff Sweet just sent a telegram off to Jacob Hooper, tellin' him you're here. Seems he saw Starr Faithful squeezin' your trigger and he's real jealous. You better git!

Scene 10

Jesse James is alone in a hotel room. Jacob Hooper answers the phone in his office.

                JESSE
              (on phone)

Jacob Hooper?

                HOOPER
              (on phone)

Yes. Who is this?

                JESSE

I'd like to give you some crime information.

                HOOPER

Call the police.

                JESSE

Concerning a threat to freedom.

                HOOPER

Of what magnitude?

                JESSE

A conspiracy.

Hooper signals for Babycakes, who enters with a dictating machine.

HOOPER
(suspicious)
I'm all ears.

JESSE
A very highly placed group of men plan to wipe out a whole segment of the nation.

HOOPER
Go on—who are the targets?

JESSE
The oldest and most established members of the country.

HOOPER
"Wipe out?" Be specific, what do you mean?

JESSE
Genocide.

HOOPER
Genocide?
(low to Babycakes)
Do we know anything about a genocide threat?
(to Jesse)
Who are the leaders?

JESSE
One of them is a man of impeccable credentials, years in government service but known for his flagrant degeneracy.

                        HOOPER

Who is this creep?

                        JESSE

Are we alone?

                        HOOPER

Yes, of course.

                        JESSE

Can I speak confidentially?

                        HOOPER

It's just between you and I—who is this prevert?

                        JESSE
                    (whispers)
You! Jacob Hooper. You and your war, you and your degeneracy!

                        HOOPER

Who is this??

                        JESSE

Jesse James, keep in touch.

       Phones slam down.

                        HOOPER
                   (to Babycakes)
Don't take that down! What's the matter with you?

They exit. Jesse speaks out.

JESSE

I had to talk to somebody.

My legs pain me deep down like toothaches. But I've seen this country, this incredible country of beauty.

I watched the Rockies from an open flatcar, freight train pushing through the summer snow, down to all the little midnight towns where people dream about goin' to the big city, wake up and find their children already gone. I do get tired alone. It's tough moving on your own steam, disturbing people who can't see the sparks before the fire. Everybody's feeling too safe to listen.
(pause)
I try to warn this country of what it's doing, but I see a thoughtless, foolish people. I started out peaceful, feel myself turning cold. A man could freeze running underground.

He exits.

Scene 11

Johnnie, Shorty, and Deafy are getting ready for the big job. Johnnie dresses carefully.

JOHNNIE

Tomorrow night there's gonna be a big bash benefittin' the Indians. Ma and her boys, Chief Flaherty, Pretty Boy, Machine Gun, Jake the Barber, Silent Margaret—the whole neighborhood's gonna be there. It's a rumor Jess James is comin' outta hiding to sing a song. We could dance and taste everything on the menu, meat and vegetables! I'll steal a diamond ring and call you my wife!

SHORTY

How many carats?

JOHNNIE

All you can eat!

SHORTY

Thanks, Johnnie. Who's driving our getaway car?

JOHNNIE

Potatoes Goldberg, best wheelman around. Drives with his right hand, shoots with his left, spits thumbtacks out his mouth. He's a pro.

DEAFY

Who's our wheels, Johnnie?

                        JOHNNIE

Potatoes.

                        DEAFY

Potatoes? He's a pro.

                        JOHNNIE
                       (to Shorty)
You gotta clear everybody out the bank before we set this thing off.

                        SHORTY

Of course, Johnnie.

                        JOHNNIE

Now, again: Potatoes stays in the seedan, Deafy covers the entrance, you and me crash. You're carryin' the boomboom. Round everybody up into the right hand corner near the savings accounts.

                        SHORTY

Checking.

                        JOHNNIE

Checking.

SONG: "EVERYBODY'S GOT A JOB TO DO"

                        JOHNNIE

Everybody's got a job to do
Successful larceny relies on absolute cooperation

Everybody's standing in his place
Larceny requires community participation.

You do this and I'll do that
You go here and I'll go there
Robbin' a bank means getting it all together.

You run here and I'll stand there
You hold the dough—I'll hold the gat
We'd best be careful—you check out the weather, Shorty.

Then we'll be riding down the street
Checking out the dump we'll hit
Everything planned—everything neat.

It means that you're in your place
Doing your job, and I'm in mine
You get the dough—I've got the gun
Head for the car—we'll have to run

I'll keep my gun trained on the people in the street
And everything works just like clockwork
Everything planned—everything neat.

I'll feel that gun
Just resting lightly on my arm
And we'll get the dough-ray-me and head right out of town
I'd like to see those cops' expression
When they look around and Johnnie's struck again.

WANTED

SHORTY

I'll do this and you'll do that
I'll go here and we'll go there together.
I'll run here and you'll stand there
I'll hold the dough—we'll rob that bank together, Johnnie.

Then we'll be riding down the street
Checking out the dump we'll hit
Everything planned—everything neat.
God, it's so exciting!

We'll deal the system a death blow
The rotten system's got to go
Working in that filthy bank
We'll feel the power of the new and coming order.

DEAFY

You do this—we'll do it all together
Everybody's got his job to do
I'll go there—we'll do it all together, kids.

Then we'll be riding down the street
Checking out the dump we'll hit
Everything planned—everything neat.

The important thing in pulling a job
Is making sure your wheels are oiled
You've got a trusty man to handle the getaway car
Yah—everything neat—everything planned
Everything tunning nice and smooth—smooth—smooth.

SONG ENDS

(Shorty hugs Johnnie.)

                    JOHNNIE
I sure am crazy about you, Shorty, and I don't mean maybe. For a college girl, you hug swell.

                    SHORTY
                (pulls away)
Don't ever call me that, Johnnie. I quit college.

                    JOHNNIE
Sure, honey, but why do—

                    SHORTY
I was a victim of privilege, the inequality of the system, same as you, same as the Indians. But I wasn't aware of it until last semester, when I withdrew.

                    JOHNNIE
And all these years I've been robbin' banks just for the fun.

                    SHORTY
Fun? Come on, Johnnie, there's a deep psychological outrage at work in every—

                    JOHNNIE
Fun! I been hearin' all that psychology lingo and I'll tell you a secret—

(whispers)
It's horseshit. What it is is fun! Why I've lived more in forty minutes at a time than my old man's lived in forty years. My mug's on every front page in the country—I'm famous, I'm a Known! A Known!

You spend days casin' a job, sittin' around drinkin' good Milwaukee beer plannin' your routes in and your routes out. You start feelin' the jumps in your gut night before and you can't sleep for nothin' thinkin' about dashin' in with your machine gun strapped to the arm, everybody gapin' at you and you're lookin' grand and so powerful. But it gets you worst slowly wheelin' into town real dignified and you keep tastin' your eggs and bacon the whole way till you get to the door. But once she starts rippin' you forget everything but gettin' the green and gettin' your ass the hell outta town without feelin' any holes in you—wonderin' how much you got in the bag, hopin' it's all twenties and fifties and no ones at all!

SONG: "GUNS ARE FUN"

JOHNNIE

When you feel blue
all you need to do is
look at a gun and laugh your blues away
'cause guns are fun
that's all there is to it
come on and do it.

When you feel sad
when you want to cry
pick up a gat

and run your fingers through it
your mood will change
from low to high
just give it a try.

I know some guys get their kicks
from gambling and broads
well, that's their point of view.
But me, I go to the store
and look at some rods
it cheers me up like nothing else can do.

So take my advice
give up those dice
give up those chicks
who want money and ice
find you a rifle
it gives you a life full
of thrills at a very low price—
nice!

And when you're alone
look at your gun
that way you'll never
need anyone
just you and your gun
will go sailing through
every wonderful fun-filled day
and kiddo—when you feel blue
all you need to do
is look at your gun

and laugh your blues away.
Oh God, it's such fun!
Gaze at your gun
and laugh your blues away.
Put your blues on the run
gawp at your gat
and laugh your blues away.
Your life will shine like the sun
stare at your gun
and laugh your blues away.

SONG ENDS

(to Shorty)

But since you come along and Jesse's been talkin' I realize how it's political, too, and endin' the Indian massacre's what's really important.

SHORTY

(daydreaming)

Right—that's what it's all about, Johnnie.

(to herself)

It is fun, goddamit, isn't it!

JOHNNIE

You better call the bank—get him the hell out fast.

SHORTY

(nods, picks up phone)

Is this the bank? I'd like to speak to President Collins. Daddy? Phyllis. Will you meet me for lunch at exactly eleven-thirty? It's really serious, Daddy. The Cheesecake Restaurant, way across town, so you better leave now. Okay, thanks, Daddy. Don't be late!

Three loud honks from a car horn. Shorty and Johnnie start moving, Deafy doesn't budge.

DEAFY

Where the hell's Potatoes? He don't get here on time the whole job's botched. You know I—

JOHNNIE

Deafy! Let's go!

DEAFY

I hear ya for chrissake, Johnnie—don't have ta holler.
(points to lunchbox bomb)
Sensitive to sound, blow the place sky-high. Know what I'm tryin' to bring out here?

They exit for the car, Deafy shaking his head.

Scene 12

Billy and Starr Faithful have been riding hard. They make their way onto a plateau.

BILLY

Okay. There's a view. I can see down the ravine, inta the canyon, inta the pass. You want some coffee?

She nods, spreads their blanket as he hands her the coffee. She winces.

BILLY

Too hot?

STARR FAITHFUL

Too sweet.

BILLY

You gotta go or anythin'?

STARR FAITHFUL

Don't worry about me.

BILLY

I didn't bring you along to not worry about you.
(looks her over)
Jeezus, you're awful dirty.

STARR FAITHFUL

What?

BILLY

I don't think I ever seen a woman so dirty. I prob'ly even give you critters by now, didn't I? Admit it! Dammit did I give you critters, are you itchin' yourself crazy 'cause of my damn infectious critters?

STARR FAITHFUL

I'm not complaining, Billy.

BILLY

Did I give you critters?

STARR FAITHFUL

Yes! You gave me critters!

BILLY

See! You're a damn mess and it's all my fault.

STARR FAITHFUL

Am I too much of a mess for you?

BILLY

No.

STARR FAITHFUL

Well then lay off!

BILLY
(shakes his head)
I even got you hollerin' like a payday hooch.

(pause)

I'm sorry. Guess it takes time knowin' how to be with somebody. I ain't never done it before, and we're tryin' to do it so cash-down fast.

(pause)

I'll tell you somethin' Starrbaby—I'm a little scairt.

STARR FAITHFUL

Billy? Scared of what?

BILLY

Gettin' kilt. I never cared much about it before you showed up. I just did things. I think you can do most anythin' when you don't care.

STARR FAITHFUL

Well, don't start being cautious because of me, it's not your way. That's how people get hurt, when they try to do things not their way, not their style.

BILLY

(sees something in distance)

Okay, yeah—

STARR FAITHFUL

So if you find yourself acting differently, tell me, and I'll leave, honestly. Of course, you'll have to give me good directions out of here, but—Billy, what's the matter?

BILLY

Only one man I know rides that way.

STARR FAITHFUL
Who? What way?

BILLY
Jacob Hooper. Sidesaddle.

He grabs his bag, forgets the coffee cups.

Scene 13

Jacob Hooper, with a bow and arrow, and Babycakes arrive at the campsite vacated by Billy and Starr Faithful.

HOOPER

Have they been gone long?

BABYCAKES

The coffee's still sweet.

Hooper nods, reaches to pick up a cup.

BABYCAKES

Don't shake it! Coffee stays sweet six hours post-sugaration. I would judge by the lumpy sediment at the posterior of the cup that they were here not more than five hours ago—according to taste.

HOOPER

I wonder who he's with.

BABYCAKES

What's our aim, Mr. Hooper? Alive? Dead? Or dead-or-alive?

HOOPER

Maimed.

Bring an Indian-lover in dead and what justice is there? Bring him in alive and he might skidaddle—I can't afford another skidaddle.

Oh, they'd love that! Showing me holding the bag, with egg on my face! What would I do then?

Where could I go?
(pause)
Maimed. A crippled man is guilty as the devil.

He exits with Babycakes.

Scene 14

Opal and SHERIFF SWEET inch towards a distant firelight.

OPAL

Sheriff Sweet, how do we know it's The Kid? I can't see a thing, we might—

SHERIFF SWEET

We'll just track 'em till we meet up with Jacob and the others. Vamonos!

They exit. Hooper and Babycakes enter, cross silently, hunting Billy.

Scene 15

Billy Enters carrying Starr Faithful. She's ill and weak. He lets her down gently, bracing her against his body. He reaches into his shirt pocket, feeds her something.

STARR FAITHFUL

What is it?

BILLY

Called peyote—it'll ease you.

She bites into it, winces, tries to hand it back to him.

It's medicine, chew.

STARR FAITHFUL
(chews)

We shouldn't stop, shouldn't build a fire, Billy.

BILLY
(takes a bite himself)

You be quiet now.

STARR FAITHFUL

Where you going??

BILLY

How you feelin'?

STARR FAITHFUL
Better. That medicine goes right to your head, doesn't it?

BILLY
Pukin' your damn guts up every morning—it's a sign, it's some kinda sign.
(holds her)
Gotta get you to a bones but there ain't no bones around here, that's for sure.

STARR FAITHFUL
I'll be okay. This is fine.

BILLY
'Magine what it would be like not havin' to run, stayin' in one place, maybe growin' corn and horses, cows, bein' part of a place. I been thinkin'—we could do it, maybe north, in Canada, you can live in Canada.

STARR FAITHFUL
That's not Billy The Kid. "You can't go changin' who you been." Who said that, hmm? You're not a farmer, you hate cows.

BILLY
Maybe.

STARR FAITHFUL
You'd be so restless—slow down and lose your spin. I wouldn't swap that spin for a hundred horses and a thousand fields of corn.

                    (grins)
I'd be so restless without it! You've been thinking a lot, haven't you?

                    BILLY
Must be the medicine.

> *Jacob Hooper and Babycakes sneak up to one side of the camp ridge. Sheriff Sweet and Opal sneak up on the other. The two groups are unaware of each other.*

                    HOOPER
Just over the ridge, I can hear them.

                    OPAL
The Kid'd never burn a fire, sheriff. It's a trap, waiting for us to crawl in. I can hear them.

                    SHERIFF SWEET
We'll circle around.

                    HOOPER
Circle around!

> *The four of them circle around.*

                    STARR FAITHFUL
Hold me, Billy.

                    OPAL
Ssh—

BABYCAKES
I can't see a thing, Mr. Hooper.

SHERIFF SWEET
Circle the other way 'round.

HOOPER
Turn around.

> *The two posses, on opposite sides of the ridge, mistake each other for Billy.*

OPAL
There they are!

HOOPER
Open up!

> *They all open fire with rubber arrows and popguns. Billy dives towards Starr Faithful, just as she jumps up in fear.*

STARR FAITHFUL
Billy!

> *He pulls her down, unaware that she's been shot with an arrow. The others keep shooting at each other across the ridge, yelling as they do.*

BILLY
(inching out of camp, pulling her by the hand)
Come on, come on! They haven't spotted us. Get up!

STARR FAITHFUL
I can't—

BILLY
For chrissake get up!

> *She tries, falls. Billy pulls her over the ridge, while the posses keep at each other.*

HOOPER
(to Babycakes)
Hold fire.
(yells across the ridge)
We got you, Kid—lay 'em down!

OPAL
Himself!

SHERIFF SWEET
Jacob, don't shoot. It's me, Sweet!

> *They are all astonished, slowly meet near the center of the extinguished fire. Billy and Starr Faithful are out of range.*

BILLY
(yanks off the rubber arrow)
I think they got you, Starrbaby.

STARR FAITHFUL
Billy, I'm—

BILLY

Ssh—don't try to sing.

STARR FAITHFUL

Promise me—

BILLY

What?

STARR FAITHFUL

Locate Mama!

BILLY
(hesitates, shrugs)

I promise. Now listen, we'll make it to a—

STARR FAITHFUL

Save yourself, Billy—I'm—dead.

BILLY
(shakes her)

SONG: "I WANT TO RIDE WITH YOU" (Reprise)

He gets up, screams and runs. Exits.

HOOPER & OTHERS

There they are!

The posse rushes up, finds Starr Faithful.

SHERIFF SWEET

Is she dead?

BABYCAKES
(kneels down to her)

She's singing.

(listens again)

She's dead.

OPAL

Where's The Kid?

HOOPER

Skidaddled.

(looks down at Starr Faithful)

She was probably a horrible person. She got in the way. Get rid of her.

Babycakes hoists her body and they exit, leaving Hooper.

HOOPER
(low voice)

Lord, I am doing my job—best I know how. There's no precedents to go on, nobody set me any examples, just thou shall not kill and like that. They're all on my back! Newspapers, magazines even the head of the damn government—I'm watching him, by the way. Between you and I he gives too much stuff to people who are lazy as the devil. He's a softie, him and his crew.

(pause)

I can't trust a soul. I see so much evil all over the place and nobody but you to tell it to. They think I'm a fanatic or something because I've got everybody's number. Well this country is full of traitors! Indian-lovers sneaking around saying it's wrong what we're doing to the Redskins. Well, I've seen the horror they've done to naked men—and women. I've seen it! And if we're not on our toes they'll take over the country just like that. They're all involved in it—each and every one of them's tied up and linked! I know it. I've got—whattayacallit—evidence! Evidence. Just let them try to get something on me. They all yell when The Kid skidaddles, but if I shoot somebody down they're crying massacre. Kill a killer with one bullet and you're doing your job, kill him with fifty and you're a butcher.

(pause)

I don't understand people. Dillinger sneaks home for a visit and all the neighbors come by to say hello. The whole town knew he was there and nobody called me! What do you have to do to be popular, kill people and rob banks? And they just love to spread rumors —I've heard them, vicious, malicious—hearsay. Well, I'm a normal person! If I don't socialize with women it's because I haven't found her yet—whoever she is. And I simply prefer the company of men. You're the only one I can trust.

(pause)

I can trust you?

(smiles)

There's a couple of things you're not so proud of, right?

> *VOICES call out his name as he stands in a beam of light. Blackout.*

END OF ACT ONE

Act Two

Scene 16

Ma Barker wears an apron, a holster and gun slung around her waist. She's reading "The Raven" to Doc and Jelly, who sit at her feet.

MA

"... Quoth the Raven, 'Nevermore'."

She begins the next verse and midway through Rabbits appears looks cautiously, then makes a dash for the door and out. The boys watch her go, smile. Ma shakes her head.

DOC

That's the fourth time she broke out since we got here.

Jelly laughs.

MA

I can count.

JELLY

She's an escape artist.

MA

Shame on the both of you! That poor woman's been though it— you'd stay'd in The Cut as long as she's done you'd be buggerin' each other for breakfast. Now settle down and finish your lesson. I'll leave a blank on the last word. You gotta fill it in, that's the test.

(reads the last verse)

"... Quoth the Raven—Blank." What's the last word?

JELLY

Blank!

DOC
(confidently)

"Not again."

MA

Close enough. "A."

(to Jelly)

"A minus."

JELLY

It's fixed. It's always fixed! You give him that answer, I saw it— you're always givin' him the answers!

MA
(slowly draws her gun)

You callin' your mother crooked?

Open the door, let her back in.

> *Angry, Jelly rises and opens the door. Rabbits is standing right there. She walks in muttering. Jelly picks up the newspaper from the doorstep.*

RABBITS

It's never quiet, it's never quiet, you're never alone ...

MA
(puts an arm over her shoulder)
That's okay, honey. Now just have a bite to eat, you can't keep escapin' on an empty stomach.

JELLY
(reading paper)
Hey Ma, lookee here, they're runnin' your mug right up front!

They crowd around him.

DOC
Gee Ma, you look like a regular lady.

JELLY
Yeah, and your mustache don't even show!

MA
(hands paper to Doc)
Read it.

DOC
What for? It always says the same damn—

MA
Read it! Hooper calls us vermins, does he? "A family of vermins."

Doc reads it, Ma paces. He hands it to Jelly who looks at it without much success. Rabbits jumps up and escapes.

DOC
I don't see why your makin' such a big deal—

MA
Shut up!

JELLY
(frightened)
What's wrong, Ma? Somethin' bad? Are we in—

MA
Nothin', Jelly honey. Why don't you go see if you can find Rabbits.

JELLY
She's standin' right outside the door, Ma, you know that.

MA
Well, take her for a walk, that's what she likes best, goin' for a walk alone. You go take her on one.

JELLY
(goes sullenly, open door, Rabbits is right there)
Come on, Rabbits.

They exit.

DOC
What's that all about?

MA

I was worried about your brother.

DOC

Oh, don't worry about Jelly, Ma. He's gettin' all A-minuses.

MA

He was bein' scared. Jelly's got delicate emotions. All my children got delicate emotions... all my children are... special... all my children are good children... all my children...

DOC
(touches her elbow)

What's the matter, Ma?

MA
(snaps out of it)

You read that damn article, Hooper's comin' after us personal. "A family of vermins." Well I got dignity!

DOC

Never mind about Hooper, Ma, he's just another rotten G-man.

MA

No. He's the plague. He's the plague. Like Jesse says, his hands are slidin' 'round the neck of this land like the grip of death, and nobody but the likes of us crooks and Indians is aware of it—cause we're on the outside feelin' the pinch before the squeeze. People inside, the good gray people, they're likin' it fine right now because all they feel is a little warm pressure. And they call that "protection." Thinkin' they're safe, like smilin' baby in the arms of a lunatic. Well, it's a plague Doc, and he's gonna squeeze out their freedom like a bloody vomit from the throat of the land— and those good gray people ain't gonna know where it went till they're in the desert on their knees droolin' red puke in the sand.

DOC

Last time I threw up was on Jelly's birthday. It was right on Jelly in fact. Remember, Ma? We wuz—

MA

All my life I brought my boys up to disrespect the law—

DOC

You done a good job, Ma.

MA

To get a sense of pride and power from your own deeds. Now a Hooper comes along, and listen Doc, there's nothin' more dangerous than a power-hungry fruit—a Hooper with so much force at his fingertips, and I gotta wonder—maybe we shoulda all been dicks.

DOC

You wasn't cut out to be a dick, Ma.

MA

Am I mean to you? Am I? I don't mean to be mean to you, Doc, I've just got such visions for my boys. I mightta been better off not bein' a career woman, but I seem to have been made that way. I couldn't bear to see you make mistakes.

DOC

Aint made a one, have I? I'm learnin' good, Ma!

SONG: "I DO THE BEST I CAN I CAN"

MA

It's not easy being a woman in this world of men
Not easy being a mother in this world of sons
Not easy being a human in this universe of beasts
But I'm tryin', I do the best I can.

I do the best I can every day
I do the best I can for everyone in every way—
Sometimes happy, sometimes sad,
But I've given all I had,
And I'm glad to say I do the best I can.

People mock and people scorn my gunslingin' ways
That's all right with me 'cause long ago I gave up seekin' praise.
No one knows another's life till he's lived it all the way
I'm happy I can say at the close of every day

I do the best I can every day
I do the best I can for everyone in every way—
Sometimes happy, sometimes sad,
But I've given all I had,
And I'm glad to say I do the best I can.

Long ago I thought that other paths were open
That's because I thought that everyone was free
But freedom's just another word for hopin'

Now I know my life's the way it had to be.

I do the best I can every day.

SONG ENDS

DOC
Aw Ma, don't be singin' such a sad song. Sing that song you and me and Jelly used to sing.

MA
You want to hear me sing that old lullaby, Doc?

DOC
Yeah, Ma,

MA
Well all right, come on over here.

SONG: "LULLABY"

The sun touches the earth
The moon touches the sea
Color touches the rose
And love touches you and me.

The lamb cries for its mammy
The grass cries for the dew
The bird cries for its mate
And my heart cries for you.

DOC

That's the one, Ma.

> *Doc sings the first verse of "Lullaby." Ma enters over him, singing "I Do the Best I Can I Can."*

MA

I do the best I can every day
I do the best I can for everyone in every way—
Sometimes happy, sometimes sad,
But I've given all I had,
And I'm glad to say I do the best I can.

SONG ENDS

> *Ma and Doc exit. Rabbits enters followed by Jelly looking around for Ma.*

RABBITS

It's never quiet, you're never alone, you're never alone, it's—

JELLY

Ma? Hey, Ma?

> *They exit. Ma and Doc enter.*

MA

But I sure can cook the ass off any regular housewife, can't I? We'll outsmart this Hooper sonofabitch, just like we done all the rest of 'em!

DOC
Now you're talkin', Ma!

They embrace. Jelly enters.

JELLY
Ma! I just knocked into Silent Margaret, she says everybody's in town and there's gonna be a big bash for the Indians tonight over the Biograph Theatre followin' the show—all music and dancin', sandwiches and East Oklahoma moonshine!

DOC
Sounds like a treat, Ma.

MA
We gotta be careful, boys, real careful now—

JELLY
It's all sweet sailin', Ma. Police Chief Flaherty's gonna be guest've honor.

MA
(spins her gun, considers)
Well, I suppose if everybody else's gonna promenade over there then—

SONG: "WAHOO"

DOC & JELLY
(chorus)
Hip diddle oo wahoo wahoo

Hip diddle oo wahoo wahoo
Hip diddle oo wahoo wahoo
Wahoo wahoo

                        JELLY

Hip diddle oo

                        DOC

Hip diddle oo
Hip diddle oo

                    DOC & JELLY

Hip diddle oo
Wahoo wahoo wa-hoo

                        DOC

What did the rooster say to the hen?

                    MA & JELLY

Wahoo wahoo

                        DOC

What did the rooster say to the hen?
We did it once, let's do it again

                        ALL

Wahoo wahoo wa-hoo
                    (sing chorus)

JELLY
What did the billy goat say to the nanny?

MA & DOC
Wahoo wahoo

JELLY
What did the billy goat say to the nanny?

MA & DOC
Wahoo wahoo

JELLY
What did the billy goat say to the nanny?
I had your ma and I had your granny

ALL
Wahoo wahoo wa-hoo

(sing chorus)

MA
What did the stallion say to the mare?

DOC & JELLY
Wahoo wahoo

MA
What did the stallion say to the mare?

DOC & JELLY
Wahoo wahoo

MA

What did the stallion say to the mare?
One is good and two is fair
Do it three times and four is right there

DOC

Five is great and six means seven
'Cause eight is just like being in heaven

JELLY

Nine ten let's do it again

ALL
(sing chorus)

SONG ENDS

JELLY
(does a little jig)
We'll come home before late, won't we, Doc?

MA

What the hell do you think I'm gonna do? Sit home and diddle myself? If we go we all go, Rabbits included.

JELLY
(low)

Aw nuts!

                    MA

You objectifying, Jelly?

                    DOC

Ma deserves some recreatin' too, don't she, Jell?

                    JELLY
                  (sullen)

Nobody else's mother'll be there.

                    MA
            (uneasy, not listening)

I'm not sure though—maybe it's too risky.
                  (pause)
I wish somebody'd assassinate that Hooper bastard like he deserves and ease my mind. Lemme think on it. Now whatta you boys want for supper? Be precise, I'm not runnin' a restaurant here.

                 DOC & JELLY

Fish! Stew! Tongue! Chops! Beef Bourguignon!

                    MA
                  (smiles)

And my nice Indian puddin' for desert?

> *She draws her gun, twirls it, lays it in her palm outwards them*

Kiss it, boys—it's your dad!

> *They kneel down as if it were customary to kiss the gun.*

Scene 17

Babycakes is tapping into a phone conversation, taking notes. He becomes fascinated and forgets to write it down.

TWO VOICES
(on phones)

—Darling.
—Don't call me that, use the code.
—Uncle Jim, how long must we keep playing this game?
—Not much longer. I'm getting a new car.
—What kind?
—Large, spacious.
—I don't want to be a back-seat girl all my life.
—You won't. It's a station wagon. I love you, Pie.
—When will you be near me, Uncle Jim?
—What are you wearing?
—Very little, my love.
—For instance?
—Socks.
—How high do they go?
—To the knee. They're knee socks.
—What else?
—Gloves.
—Gloves?

Jacob Hooper has walked in and has been listening too.

HOOPER

Babycakes!

Babycakes jumps up.

I leave you alone for five minutes and you get involved in that drivel?

BABYCAKES

Forgive me, Mr. Hooper! I was daydreaming. I've developed a method of daydreaming and concentrating at the same moment.

HOOPER

Quiet! How am I to believe you're happy working with me when I find you drooling over smut?

BABYCAKES

I'm ecstatic, Mr. Hooper!

HOOPER

Don't lie to me!

BABYCAKES

Never!

HOOPER

Don't forget you are a tool and that every tool can be replaced, and every tool can be broken.

BABYCAKES

Please don't frighten me, Mr. Hooper.

He's on the verge of tears when Opal comes in.

OPAL

Excuse me, Jacob. Is this private?

HOOPER

It's never private. Where have you been? The Barkers just killed a nice sheriff in Texas.

OPAL

Jacob, they took the bait!

HOOPER

Good!
    (thinks)

What bait?

OPAL

The Benefit Ball for the Indians. All the bandits have come to town.

HOOPER

When?

OPAL

Tomorrow night. Every big name in the business.

HOOPER

This is what we've been waiting for! Call Flaherty, the police chief.
    (she calls)
A Bandits' Ball. I wonder what I should wear. Is it costume?

OPAL

He's unavailable.

HOOPER

What? Then we'll have to handle this ourselves for now. And I'm warning you, one more botch and the whole batch of you are in deep trouble.

OPAL

I just heard Dillinger knocked off another bank.

HOOPER

Enough bad news! You get down there, make arrangements. Try to buy tickets, reserve me a corner hotel room with a fancy hot plate, three extra soft pillows and a large bed.

OPAL

How large?

HOOPER

A queen!

Babycakes.

Opal exits.

BABYCAKES
(rattled)

Yes, Mr. Hooper?

                    HOOPER
Don't be upset with me.

                    BABYCAKES
I'm afraid I've failed you.

                    HOOPER
No. You've only let me down a smidgen, a technical error. Failure is bigger—it's—in a glance. Come sit down.
                    (pats his knee)
I'll apologize in your ear.

                    BABYCAKES
                    (sits on his knee)
But I hesitate to exonerate myself—

                    HOOPER
Quiet! Whisper to me.

SONG: "WHISPERING TO YOU"

                BABYCAKES & HOOPER
Whispering words to your associate in business
Makes the day seem much more pleasant in every way
Whispering words creates a lovely feeling
At the close of every busy, work-fillled day.

                    BABYCAKES
Whispering the things he wants to hear about himself
Telling him he's brave and strong
Ready to meet every crisis

HOOPER

If everyone could see me now
Those folks who say I'm cold as ice
'Tis clear that they would realize
That I'm a tender, warm-hearted man.

BABYCAKES & HOOPER

And I do [he does] the best I [he] can
Whispering thoughts we cannot voice before the others
We can talk about the weather, public duties, and our mothers

BABYCAKES

It makes all the difference, Mr. Hooper.

HOOPER

Babycakes, you know that I enjoy it, too.

BABYCAKES & HOOPER

It gives the end of the day a satisfaction
That nothing else could ever give or do

BABYCAKES

But let's be honest, it's not just the action

BABYCAKES & HOOPER

It's because I'm whispering to you
It's because I'm whispering to you

SONG ENDS

Scene 18

Johnnie, Shorty and Deafy enter, cross carefully to the bank, their guns concealed. Shorty carries the bomb.

SHORTY
(turns, talks to Potatoes, unseen)
Potatoes keep the doors open! Keep the motor going. Don't forget—

JOHNNIE
Quiet! Potatoes has been around, you are new, keep your yap shut.

SHORTY
Right. Listen, Johnnie, maybe we shouldn't all walk so suspiciously. I mean what if we all sort of—sauntered over there—like this—

She juggles the bomb.

JOHNNIE
Careful with that!
(reaches, takes it)
Gimme the bomb!

SHORTY
Oh, I'm sorry, Johnnie—it's just so exciting! I'm doing it, aren't I—I'm really involved!

SONG: "I WANT TO BLOW UP THE WORLD"

I want to blow up the world
I want to show up the world
for what it is
but before I do, world,
I have some things I want to say to you, world.

I don't love you any more
the way you cheat the good, the poor
your scheming hands around their throats
your favorite word is dispossess.

I don't love you anymore
'cause to love you is to be your whore
and spend your live giving more and more
for less and less.

World, I don't love you anymore
look at your record, world,
look what you've done
you've used a handful of gold to blot out the sun
and who's to blame?
You know your name—
world, you're the one.

The emptiness of the middle class
the boredom of the rich
I hate you, you sonofabitch.

Don't try to sweet-talk me, world,

don't think that rivers and moons
and children and balloons
and mommy and daddy and chocolate ice cream
and individual liberties and being nice and kind
will change my mind.

World, you're way behind
I've learned another way to live
I'm becoming a poor girl at last
no poor little rich girl any more
Johnnie's teaching me and I'm learning fast.

I live in one room
I run from the cops
I never take a bath
drink water from the tap
I'm learning the slang
handling a gun
cooking up grub
I've even had the clap
I've become a real member of the proletariat
I'm just plain folks like you, Johnnie, aren't I?
I mean ain't I.

I want to blow up the world
see it all explode in the air
all dirt and corruption disappear in that beautiful glare
and then the world will be clean again, fresh again.
Johnnie is Adam, I am Eve
just Johnnie and me in some Eden of ideological purity.

I'm going to blow up the world
one blast, one glare
and my guilt will vanish in the clear fresh air.

So goodbye world—au revoir!
You never did much for me.
I'm going to blow up the world—
then maybe I'll be free.

SONG ENDS

Scene 19

Deafy and Johnnie are counting their money. A silence.

DEAFY
(looks up)
What?

JOHNNIE
Nothin'!

DEAFY
I lost the count. Gotta count all over again! Next time you got nothin' to say—keep it to yourself. Now I gotta count this all over again, you know what I'm tryin' to bring out here?

Shorty enters.

SHORTY
Almost time for the ball, Johnnie.

A knock on the door. Shorty and Johnnie look up, Deafy keeps counting. It's followed by a series of knocks. At the final knock, Johnnie nods.

JOHNNIE
Somebody's at the door.

He puts his money away. Shorty opens the door. Deafy keeps counting. Billy enters, dusty, tired.

BILLY
(distantly)

Johnnie home?

SHORTY

Hey, that's a great outfit! Johnnie, somebody from the ball.

JOHNNIE

I'm Johnnie.

BILLY

I'm Billy The Kid. My Starrbaby's dead.

JOHNNIE

Gollee! Welcome, welcome to our little dump.

BILLY

Can you gimme shelter? I been told you could.

JOHNNIE

What a surprise—sure, sure. How long you been on the lam?

BILLY

On the what?

JOHNNIE

How long you been runnin'?

BILLY

Fifty years.

SHORTY

You must be exhausted! Sit down.

JOHNNIE

Where you comin' from?

BILLY

Wild west.

JOHNNIE
(slaps his forehead)

Whatta question.

BILLY

My Starrbaby's dead.

SHORTY

Your who's what?

JOHNNIE
(motions her to be quiet)

What are you runnin' from, Billy?

BILLY

Hooper. Hooper kilt my baby.

SHORTY

Establishment rat bastard.

JOHNNIE

How'd she die?

SHORTY
Yeah, how did she die? I mean was—

Johnnie shoves her out of the way, right into Deafy, still counting. He looks up, sees Billy, goes for his gun—

DEAFY
(clutches his money)
Oh no, you don't!

Billy shoots him with a powder gun. Deafy has a delayed reaction—falls.

JOHNNIE
Deafy!

They run to his side.

DEAFY
It's... it's noon! Noon's when there's no shadows.

BILLY
(looks closely)
Uncle Jeb??

DEAFY
Billy—Billy boy—

Shorty and Johnnie gape at them.

BILLY

Uncle Jeb, where the hell you been?

DEAFY

Johnnie, he's okay, he's all right, reminded me of you. You haven't aged much, son.

BILLY

Hooper's on my trail. Hooper shot my baby.

DEAFY
(in pain)

Oooh—

BILLY

Now don't go dyin' on me, Uncle Jeb!

DEAFY

Billy, Billy, Billy boy—long time—no—see.

He dies. Johnnie takes the money out of Deafy's hand.

JOHNNIE
(sadly)

Such a motiveless, non-political death.

BILLY
(taking it from him)

Such a load of horseshit.

A tense moment.

SHORTY

Hey, Johnnie, we're gonna miss the ball.

JOHNNIE

Good thinkin', Shorty. Oh, this here is Shorty Kinder, my wife.

SHORTY
(pumping Billy's hand)

It's an enormous pleasure to shake hands with such a reputation.

JOHNNIE

Pay no mind to Shorty, she's educated.

BILLY

My Starrbaby's dead.

SHORTY

Maybe Billy would like to come with us. You might find who you're searching for.

JOHNNIE

Everybody'll be there.

BILLY
(nods, dazed)

What about Uncle Jeb?

JOHNNIE

Deafy? Nah—Deafy hates to dance—can't hear the music. Know what I'm tryin't bring out here? Stone deaf!

They exit.

Scene 20

Jacob Hooper and Babycakes arrive in town. Babycakes stands close beside Hooper, assisting him.

HOOPER
Babycakes!

BABYCAKES
Right here, sir.

HOOPER
Oh. I thought you walked off. Don't walk off. This is a strange, alien, alien town.

BABYCAKES
Why?

HOOPER
Because I'm not sure what to expect. Don't wander. Do you hear me? We've got to be on my guard!

BABYCAKES
Yes, Mr. Hooper.

HOOPER
Was I yelling? I don't want to be yelling at you.

Opal comes up behind them, unseen.

OPAL

Jacob!

Hooper grabs Babycakes, ducks behind him, spins around—

HOOPER
(as he spins)

You're under arrest!
(sees who it is)
Don't ever sneak up on me like that! What's the matter with you? You scared this boy half to death.

OPAL

Sorry, Jacob. Well, whatta you think?

HOOPER
(thinks)

About what?

OPAL

The Biograph Theatre—there it is.

HOOPER

I know that. It's very nice, very pretty—baroque, I'd say late nineteenth century.

OPAL

This is where the bandits hold their balls.

                    HOOPER
They what?

                    OPAL
Tonight. The Indian Benefit Ball.

                    HOOPER
Why do you think we've been standing here? Where's the blueprints?

                    OPAL
Unavailable.

                    HOOPER
Think we could take a quick peek inside?

                    OPAL
The decor committee won't allow visitors.

                    HOOPER
Really? Who's chairman?

                    OPAL
Bugsy Moran and Blanch Barrow, co-chairmen.

                    HOOPER
                  (impressed)
Sounds like a nice affair. Could you get tickets?

                    OPAL
Sold out.

HOOPER

I shouldn't wonder. We'll have to use my intuition. Hmm. You'll stand here. You'll go over there and me way back behind, somewhere off to the left—totally exposed. Chief Flaherty and his men will back us up. That should cover it.

OPAL

Flaherty's going to the ball.

HOOPER

What? The chief of police going to a—
(smiles)
He must have something up his sleeve.

Jelly and Rabbits walk by.

HOOPER

How do.

JELLY

How do.
(to Rabbits, low)
That there is Lucky Luciano, outta Chicago. Wait'll I tell Ma! Lucky Luciano!

They exit.

OPAL

They sure looked familiar, didn't they?

HOOPER

I like to see polite, well-mannered youth. What's the word from whatshername?

OPAL

Alistine is still playing Rabbits with Ma Barker's gang, last I heard.

HOOPER

Good. They'll all be here tonight, too.

OPAL

Shall we go, Jacob?

HOOPER

I would like to have a nap, not a lengthy nap, just enough for a dream. I'll dream about taking a very, long nap and I'll wake up refreshed.
(to Babycakes)
Lead on!
(to Opal)
You stay here. Note who comes in, who goes out and who doesn't appear at all. Phone me every hour. This is my chance! I'll break these bandits' balls once and for all! Babycakes—Babycakes, wait for me!

Scene 21

The Indian Benefit Ball.

JOHNNIE'S VOICE

Friends! Brothers and sisters of the oppressed, welcome! Welcome. Your distinguished co-chairmens have asked me to relay this message: We got no lights tonight.
(Happy sounds, whistles)
Word's out that we're bein' mingled with—but you all know the handshake. Now, even though you can't tell it we got a helluva nice buncha balloons and pretty ribbons around the place so I wanna hear it for the decor committee!
(Scattered cheers)
Okay. Enjoy yourselves, greet one another, dance, eat—food's to your left, orchestra's to your right, have a time and leave your donations for our Indian friends in the bandstand box. Oh—and please be gentlemen!

SONG: "THE BANDITS' BENEFIT BALL IN THE DARK"

—Hello Thelma, you sure look swell
—Hello Machine-Gun, things are great

—Hello Sukie, things are great
—Hello Jelly, you sure look swell

—Hello Bugsy, you sure look swell,
—Hello Shorty, things are great

—Hello Margaret, things are swell
—Hello Reverend, you sure look great

—Hello Lucky, you sure look swell
—Hello Blanche, things are great

—Hello Ziggy, things are well
—Hello Doc, things are great

JOHNNIE
(to a friend)

... They're fine, just fine. No, I ain't been back in ages—can't do it. I write 'em, you know, try to stay in touch. Yeah, they been watchin' the house like a hawk, just like hawks. I stay in touch. Sure, a little homesick, little lonesome, whatta you gonna do?

—Hello Johnnie, you sure look swell
—Hello Frenchie, things are swell

—Hello Potatoes, things are great
—Hello Buck, you sure look swell

—Hello Billy you sure look swell
—Hello Frank, things are great

—Hello Ma, things are swell
—Hello Mack, you sure look great

—Hello Clyde, you sure look great
—Hello Floyd, things are swell

—Hello Chief, things are great
—Hello Bonnie, you sure look swell

ALL

Things are great!
You sure look swell!
You sure look swell!
Things are great!

SONG ENDS

> *They all dance and move around the floor. Hooper, Babycakes, and Opal, well-armed, appear outside. Hooper signals them into position, which after some confusion they assume. Inside the ballroom the music stops. Johnnie stands on a platform.*

JOHNNIE

I been asked to make a grand announcement. One man's arrived tonight in secret, who's suffered more than most everybody for what we believe in. He risked his most blessed ass to come talk to us.
(pause)
You know who I mean! And we finally got a light!

> *Spotlight. Cheers. Jesse appears on the platform.*

JESSE

I don't mind suffering along with my friends! My friends, my friends, oh how I've missed my friends! Three of our brothers have been caught by Hooper—

(distressed voices)

They will survive! Have faith. Have faith in the Lord, have faith in yourselves! The Lord is my light and my salvation, whom shall I fear?

(pause)

The roads of this land are rutted and steep but they lead to the people. I've walked them. I've ridden them. And though the plague be on us now, I've met the people and they are clear as water. They are fresh as water at the top of the mountain. They are strong as water down the side of the mountain. They are strong as waves! We will wash away this plague.

(pause)

These men. This Hooper. God's bow is bent with wrath. The arrow ready at the string. Justice bends the arrow at their hearts, Justice strains the bow. And it is nothing but the mere pleasure of God that keeps the arrow from being drenched with their blood!

(pause)

We live in a land of troubled time And we've got to find a way. The grapes of wrath have grown again And the spring is running red. Have faith. Don't be counseled by smooth concern There's horror on the land The beast has snapped his chain And we've got to live like animals. Have faith. They'll hunt us in the caves and trees They'll try to smoke us out, persevere my friends. Have faith. The beast is clothed in the finest fur, He creeps with the softest feet. His breath is the breath of death and He looks so groomed , so clean, so white. Have faith. You know what it's all about You must know what it's all about! Have faith. The Lord is my light and my salvation; whom shall I fear?

> *His light goes out. There is the sound of confusion, then silence. Hooper and company are alert, waiting outside.*

HOOPER

There they are. You're under arrest! Fire at will, men—

They shoot spark guns, cap pistols, smoke guns. Opal rushes into the ballroom

OPAL

It's empty! They've escaped, all gone!

HOOPER

Gone?

BABYCAKES

We got this one redskin-mother-lover anyway, Mr. Hooper.

They examine a body.

HOOPER

Chief Flaherty!

BABYCAKES

A cop!

HOOPER

Flaherty, Flaherty where'd they all go??

FLAHERTY
(as he dies)

The—back—door!

HOOPER
There was a back door?

BABYCAKES
It stands to reason, Mr. Hooper, if there was a front door, then—

HOOPER
Arrrhhhh! Scour the streets! Burn the buildings! Fire down this town! I want them dead tonight!

Scene 22

A dark, empty room. Johnnie come busting in, Jesse right behind him, Billy behind Jesse.

JOHNNIE
(checks the room)

No shades. I never heard of a hideout with no shades. I'm sorry, Jesse, you shouldn't have to be in such a bum haven.

JESSE

Makes no difference.

JOHNNIE

We'll be okay here, though. Who ever thought it would come to this, burnin' a whole town 'cause of an Indian ball?

JESSE

I did.

JOHNNIE

Really? Hell, Jesse you shouldda tole somebody.

JESSE

I have. Nobody listened.

JOHNNIE

I listened! Some of them crooks didn't listen, but I listened. I always liked what you got to say, Jesse—I know what you're talkin' about—the war and all that.

BILLY

My Starrbaby's dead.

JESSE

Who's this, Johnnie?

JOHNNIE

Him? That's Billy The Kid. I wonder where in hell Shorty's at.

JESSE

Billy, Billy it's Jesse.

BILLY

Hello Jesse, my baby's dead. I'm huntin' for her Mama now, you seen her Mama? Hmm?

JESSE

I've been looking for my own Mama seventy-five years.

JOHNNIE

She was right next to us comin' out the door. She don't even know this place.
(pause)
Nobody knows this place 'cept Deafy, and he's ice cold.
(pause)
They could burn us down if they find us, Jesse. Hooper could.

JESSE

He could.

JOHNNIE

Boys, we might have to battle outta here if Hooper makes a try. Jesse, what about it, that non-violence of yours could get a man killed, you know.

JESSE

It's over.

JOHNNIE
(tosses him a gun)

That's Jesse James!

BILLY

I'll kill Hooper with my teeth. I'll chew off his hairy ears so he hears me comin'. I'll chew up his pink eyeballs so he sees me comin'. I'll chew a hole in his fat neck till that little white heart floats out—till he feels it breakin' up in my mouth.

JOHNNIE

So, you really got it in for Hooper?

JESSE
(looks out window)

No reason it should come to that. Nobody else knows about this place, Johnnie?

JOHNNIE

Not a soul.

> *Ma Barker comes sailing in, slides across the floor as she does.*

MA

Don't shoot, boys!

JOHNNIE

Ma Barker!

MA

Made it.

(rises, dusts off)

Thought I'd find you cocksuckers here. Nice speech, Jesse. You give 'em hell. We ain't never met formal. I can hardly see you now. Lemme light this candle—

JOHNNIE

Where'd you get it?

MA

Get it? I made it. I make all my candles. Like I was sayin' we aint never met formal, but I brought my sons up on your teachin's, you and Edgar Allan the poet. Hunt around for a match, will you, Johnnie? Who's the boy?

JOHNNIE

Billy The Kid.

MA

Hello there, Billy.

BILLY

My Starrbaby's dead.

MA

Sorry to hear that, Billy. I lost a little girl and a little boy myself, many years back. Too many. Prettiest little kids in the world. I run off with an Indian chief. Part Indian myself you know, Chippewa, twenty-five proof. Like I said, run off with a chief—strong as an oak, quiet as stone, sharp as a tomahawk. I loved him.

(Johnnie lights match)

Thanks, Johnnie. What was your baby's name, Billy?

BILLY

Starr Faithful Brown, she was my girl.

Jesse stares at him. Pause, then simultaneously—

JESSE

Starr Faithful Brown? She was my sister!

MA

Starr Faithful Brown? She was my daughter!

A beat.

JESSE

Mama?

MA

Randolph!

They embrace.

BILLY
(looks heavenward)
I found her Starrbaby.

MA
How'd she die, Billy?

BILLY
Died singin'.

MA
She did have a sweet little voice.

BILLY
Shot by Hooper.

MA & JESSE
Hooper!

JOHNNIE
(at the window)
Sshhh!

He snuffs out the candle.

Scene 23

Hooper is on the phone, Babycakes by his side. They wear hardhats, stand in a makeshift headquarters directing the search. Opal enters.

OPAL

An old, skinny lady snuck through. She's got information for Jacob Hooper only.

HOOPER

I hate old skinny ladies.

BABYCAKES

What's the nature of her knowledge?

HOOPER

Don't contradict me! You keep doing that, Babycakes. Quiet! If I hadn't listened to you we'd have them all, all of them—in pieces at my feet.

OPAL

She says she knows the whereabouts of Dillinger, James, Ma Barker, and The Kid.

HOOPER

Show her in.

Rabbits enters, takes off her dark glasses and dress to reveal Alistine, in shorts.

ALISTINE
I was being followed.

OPAL & BABYCAKES
Alistine!

Jelly enters, gun drawn.

JELLY
Rabbits? Rabbits my eye! Death to Jacob Hooper!

Hooper turns and shoots him with a rubber dart gun. He falls. Alistine rushes to him, pulls off the dart.

ALISTINE
Jelly, Jelly you shouldn't have followed me here!

JELLY
(beckons her close)
"Nevermore."

ALISTINE
"A," Jelly. You died with an "A."

He smiles, dies.

HOOPER
Come on! Where are they hiding?

ALISTINE
I'll tell, Mr. Hooper, but I've got something to say first.

HOOPER

Spill it.

ALISTINE

Ma Barker's a woman's woman and an all-star mom. She's good people and so are her friends. They just see things in a different light. Don't kill her, give her a chance.

HOOPER

Where are they?

ALISTINE

231 Daggit, top floor.

HOOPER

Which door?

ALISTINE

First on the right. I'll take you.

HOOPER

No thanks.

He shoots her with a water pistol. She drops.

OPAL

Jacob, she helped you.

HOOPER

If you don't like it you can join her.

BABYCAKES
Why did you do it, Mr. Hooper?

HOOPER
(softly)
I had no choice.

Scene 24

Ma, Jesse, Johnnie, and Billy are in the hideout. There is a red glow from the town burning all around them.

JESSE
Seek ye our face oh Lord, Jacob Hooper burns the night!

MA
These fire, these fires. My babies are alive and dead, my babies are dyin' and I'm so tired from the chase, so tired runnin' to the wars. These fires—these fires—

JOHNNIE
Shorty? Can you hear me? Remember what you told me about ESP and that? Shorty? I forgot how it works—whatta I have to do? I can't hear at all, not a thing. I'm gonna try real hard to get in touch.

BILLY
I got it done.
(laughs)
Got nothin' left to find, got nothin' holdin' on. Don't care if I live or die right now. I could kill the world. I'm a free man—feel free as—feel free as me!

JOHNNIE
Can't hear a thing, Shorty. What should I do again? I'm listenin'.

MA

Tired from the chase, tired from Hooper, so tired runnin', runnin'—

JESSE

If I could make them see. If I could make them see and not just feel. If they could understand why this is happening, why this should not happen when it happens. So they will know what's being done to us, know what we've been dying about.

JOHNNIE

It's too quiet—too quiet! Whatta I have to do?

JESSE

Over? Over? Somebody hear that voice saying the war's over? No?
    (laughs)
No, must've been the voice of reason.

MA

These fires—these fires—

THEY SING

JESSE

The Lord is my light and my salvation, whom shall I fear?

JOHNNIE

When you feel blue, all you have to do is look at a gun and laugh your blues away.

MA
I do the best I can every day, I do the best I can for everyone in every way.

BILLY
I want to ride with you, through the shadow of your trails.

ALL
These fires will never let us be the same!

SONG ENDS

HOOPER
This is Jacob Hooper! We know what's up there—you! All four of you vermin. And you got no way out. No fancy backdoor stuff here! I'll make you a deal, no one'll get hurt—

BILLY
(smiles)
We got nothin' to lose.

MA
Keep jawin', Hooper!

HOOPER
Let me come up and talk. I'll come alone, unarmed.

MA
(checks with others, who nod; Johnnie cocks his gun)
Nothin' crooked now, Johnnie. Okay, come on up, Hooper!

HOOPER
(low to Babycakes and Opal)
Follow me. Wait outside the door until you hear me say—God bless—twice—God bless, then come in shooting.

He knocks on the door.

MA
Keep your hands out in front of you, and move real slow.

Hooper opens the door. He enters cautiously. It's dark.

HOOPER
Who am I talking to?

MA
Ma Barker and we're all listenin'.

HOOPER
You can surrender, every one of you. No gunfire, fair trial and everything. My word of honor.

Jesse, Billy and Johnnie all snort a laugh.

MA
Quiet boys.
(to Hooper)
You couldda sang that pretty song from down below.

HOOPER

I had to prove I meant it by coming up. I'll turn around slowly—I want to talk to you straight.

He turns, sees Ma and gasps. Love music bursts forth.

MA

What's the matter, you never seen a mustache before?

HOOPER

It's happened! It's finally, finally happened!

JOHNNIE

He's nuts.

MA

Ssh! What's happened? Quiet gapin' at me like that—

HOOPER

Love! Oh my God, Ma Barker, my parasol lady! You're not like your mug shot at all! I love you instantly. You're the first woman I've ever said that to. I do—you're magnificent! I love you. I love you, oh my God. I'm in love with a woman! Do you hear me, it's love! And it's a woman!

SONG: "IT'S LOVE"

In love with a woman at last
My God, it can happen so fast!

Warmth where there'd only been heat

Reception instead of a boomerang thrust
Willing to live—willing to die
To be made into dust
A quiet voice—a steady light
And the light shines into me, inside me as far as I can see
And the voice says, "Everything is all right."

Not loving women, Ma, I always hated men
So I chased them and killed them
Left alone with dead men again and again
Dead me and me—could anything be sadder?
Ah, Ma, ma, you don't understand
But it doesn't matter, Ma,
Just come with me and take my hand
To be loved, to love me, you don't have to understand,
Just come with me and take my hand.

SONG ENDS

Ma, come away from all these—pistols. I'll set them free right now, I can do it. I have the power to do anything I wish. It's my country. I'll leave law n' order for good, we'll go to—Romania! You can all go free, free! And I'll apologize for everything bad I've ever done. Ma, will you come with me? I think I can make someone happy.

MA
(flattered, nervous)

You'd be disappointed, Jacob.

HOOPER
Nonsense! Think of what it means to them—freedom. Your sacrifice wouldn't be so great for that, would it?

JOHNNIE
Man's got a point, Ma.

JESSE
We've been fighting this creep all our lives, Ma, what about your principles?

BILLY
(smiles)
He kilt my baby. I'll chew his nose off if you gimme the word.

HOOPER
I love you! Come with me.

JOHNNIE
Say yes!

JESSE
Say no!

BILLY
Say chew!

SONG: "AS I'M GROWING OLDER"

MA
Say yes, say no, say chew,

I don't know what to do
One damning possibility
Overrides the rest
Something I've hoped for
To myself alone confessed.

To live with someone
As I'm growing older
To spend the rest of my days
And not be alone
It's more than I hoped for
More than I dreamed would ever happen to me—
To share with someone
The last burning rays of the sun.

To live with you
As we're growing older
And we could do
The normal things that old folks do
We'll sit and reminisce
About the bastards we've known
We'll listen to the gramophone
And it won't say Ma but Mrs. Hooper on my tombstone.
Jacob, I want to grow old with you.

Jacob sings the following while Ma repeats the chorus.

HOOPER

I love you, Ma,
You make me feel so happen.
I'm going to be a normal man at last.

I love a woman—it can happen so fast.
We'll do anything we want to
We'll sit and reminisce about the bastards we've known
I can steal a kiss
We'll listen to the gramophone.
Ma, Ma, I love you so much,
Ma, Ma, with you.

They dance.

SONG ENDS

JOHNNIE
Let's take our chances, get a fair trial. Whatta you say, Jesse?

He sneezes.

HOOPER
(dancing with Ma)
God bless you.

JESSE
There's no such thing, Johnnie. I run!

He turns for the door

BILLY
(draws his gun)
What's the difference? Let's die young.

Johnnies sneezes again.

                    HOOPER
                 (still dancing)
Gezundheit.

> *He immediately realizes what he's said. A moment of silence—nothing happens and he's relieved, smiles... then Babycakes and Opal rush in, shooting. They drop Jesse near the door. Opal nails Johnnie and Billy gets Opal just as she shoots him. Babycakes sees Ma with her arms around Hooper's neck and fires into her back.*

                    HOOPER
No!

> *Ma crumples at his feet. In a fury, Hooper shoots Babycakes.*

> *It's over. It has been the first sound of real gunfire.*

> *Silence.*

> *Hooper stands alone, stunned. His eyes try to comprehend the scene. He goes to Babycakes, stands over him in terrible confusion.*

                    HOOPER
Jacob Hooper loved the woman in this man.
                 (bends down over Babycakes)
Where was I? Any messages? Hmm? I am Jacob Hooper. I am lonely Jacob Hooper. No one stops—me?

(rises)

I am Himself! I am champion of the legions of justice! Noise? A noise? Somebody here?

(pause, sings)

I am the law!
I am the law!
I am the law!

Lights fade slowly on Hooper, frozen, gun in hand. The company sings "I DO THE BEST I CAN" (Reprise).

THE END

THEY TOLD ME
YOU CAME THIS WAY

THEY TOLD ME YOU CAME THIS WAY

was first performed in May 1968 at Branford College, Yale. It was directed by Michael Posnick with the following cast:

    Alex   Ken Howard
    Peter   Peter Cameron

The play was revived in the fall of 1968 for the Yale Repertory Theatre season. Mr. Posnick directed the following cast:

    Alex   Peter Cameron
    Peter   Henry Winkler

THEY TOLD ME YOU CAME THIS WAY

A cell. Two cots, one pillow.

MUSIC: Oscar Brown Jr.'s "Brother Where Are You?"

The lights come up gradually. As the music fades out, PETER drums on the cot and then the floor. It gets louder and more intricate, and lasts until ALEX can take it no longer.

ALEX

I will die of boredom long before they get here! I might die of boredom durin' my next piss. They know how to work on a man's brain all right, when there's a brain.

It's a lovely game, lovely, but they won't find me crackin'.

Wait? I'll wait. Whatever they want, I'll wait.

Jamie? I'd scratch all those victories, all but the one last Fourth. Never was a better one. You got good speed kid, no kick though, never showed me a kick. I hope you had one hidin', hope you all had one hidin'. One last kick.

He looks at the fingers of his right hand.

Two. I'd give 'em two. Two not to wait. Either way I'd give 'em two. Either way.

Alex notices Peters watching him.

Time yet? You think it's time yet? Hmmm?

He shakes his head.

Why not? How can I tell just like that without even thinkin' about it? I can tell.

(silence)

Wish I could tell you how I could tell? Got a watch or something you don't know about?

(grins)

Clock out there?

Peter gets up, Alex stands, blocking his path.

Sit down.

Peter sits, then jumps up and looks out the window.

There's no clock.

Peter goes back to his cot.

Hey.

Is it here yet?

(imitating Peter)

"Here yet?" Course not.

"What kind of question is that, you know it's not here yet, what are you asking me a question like that for?"

That's how I know it's not time. What'd they do to your tongue?

"Oh, I've got a tongue, problem is it weighs six pounds, it's hard to manage."

Peter starts to speak. Alex raises his hand.

Not another word.

World's full of tongues, six-pounders ain't cheap, all makin' music but one more'll just make noise. Couldn't hear ourselves think then could we?

Could we!

Be a real shame to waste all this nice quiet. Best to keep good care of our tongues. "I keep mine clean, scrub her every morning, shine her up by hand, stuff her right back in."

You're a cautious little bastard, hoardin' your tongue.

Peter tries to speak again.

Quiet! Don't let it out. I got hunger pains!

You could tour with a tongue like that, tour all round the world displayin' it for a profit.
(laughs)
"How am I going to make a tour dead?"

And that's not a bad question. I think you should bequeath it. Must be somebody you love could use a handsome tongue—to remember you by.

Might make themselves a little fortune too. I'd tour with that tongue.

Think of all the people I'd meet.

Only I'm in here too!

But I do hate to see a good tongue go to waste.

>*Peter tries to say something.*

Shut the fuck up.

You might want to watch out for that grandpa roach—
>*(slowly)*
Makin' a sharp left turn around—

>*Peter watches him point.*

Your shoulder.

>*Peter jumps up and swats himself.*

Kneel Ear!

>*Peter stops swatting. Alex picks up the roach, extending it towards Peter, who flinches.*

Make a wish?

>*Peter backs off. Alex chases him with the roach, stops. Alex is about to stomp on it when he changes his mind, and drops it through a hole in the floor.*

I would bet you hate roaches.

"You killed him, didn't you?"
> *(laughs)*

Me?
> *(shakes his head)*

I squeezed him through.

"He could turn right around, come back in!"

Could. But I guess he's doin' some crawlin' if he's a roach with any sense.

> *Silence. The sound of a door opening, shutting; then the close crack of gunfire. Peter screams a short scream.*

Maybe they like hearin' you scream. Your guts'll drip plenty soon, don't be droolin' 'em all over me!
> *(pauses, grunts a laugh)*

Scared of roaches. What ain't you scared of, little man?

> *Alex turns to Peter, makes a horrible face and imitates Peter's scream.*

Boo! You got that. Goddam boo!

And if you keep slobberin' on me I will pop your backbone. I will set my knee on your spine and I will snap you! Snap you like rotten kindlin'. So help me—if they don't come soon. So help me.

> *Peter picks up the pillow and throws it at Alex. They have a pillow fight. And then a mattress fight.*

How long we been here, you know?

> *Peter looks up questioningly. Alex works himself into a slow anger.*

Four days.

"Four days, you sure?"

Seems longer, right? You bet we been here longer than four days.

How do I know it's four days?

It's four days, dammit! I been scratchin' it out every mornin'.

> *Peter gets up, moves towards Alex.*

"I could scratch too, couldn't I?" That what you're thinkin'?
> *(rises)*

Well, you can do whatever you want to do, over there.

> *Alex pushes him violently back against the wall.*

You stay over there! You can scratch your back or you can scratch your nuts but you stay the hell over there!

It's four! I told you that, if you don't believe me, ask him when he brings it.

Peter gets up slowly.

"You hurt me. You hurt my back."

If you wanted to see so bad you shoulda asked for a invitation. A formal invitation's the only way you can ever get over here.

"You hurt my back." I'll snap it next time.

Silence. Peter cries softly.

Stop cryin'.

Please stop cryin'. Stop!

You won't get me that way, no you won't! I can take it! No leaky-assholed son-of-bitch is goin' to get to me, you hear that!
    (laughs a short laugh)
Next thing you'll be soundin' like him, yellow as puke, one long stream of squash puke with clothes on. There's somethin' unnormal about you boy, somethin' real unnormal.
    (pause)
But little man keep cryin', you flood this pit, go ahead.
    (laughs)
I can swim.

Rebecca, you could stop him, you could make him smile, Rebecca, even him, Rebecca, even this little drain of puke, you'd do it somehow.
    (pause)
Don't cry.

(silence)

Cryin's not gain' to help any, far as I can tell.

He lifts Peter up and walks him around the room.

You can talk yourself out of cryin'. Give it a try. Tears drown the brain, that's a fact.

Peter looks up, blows his nose.

Think about it. You ever been able to figure anything out when you blow your nose? No. Course not. Nobody can. Once had a cousin, they called him Slow, I called him Dumb, did nothin' but blow his nose. Till one mornin' found him lyin' dead, hankachif all thick and soggy in his hand, and green. Blew his brains out, only nobody knew it. They just never could understand why a kid was so dumb with a head twice the size of normal. Old Steven must of had plenty of brains though, cause it took him ten years to get rid of 'em. Family tragedy.

Peter laughs softly.

What's yours?

PETER

My what?

ALEX:

Name.

PETER

Peter.

ALEX
(nods)

What a ya think of Alex?

PETER

Nice.

ALEX

Not goin' to cry again are you?

Peter shakes his head. Silence.

ALEX

It won't get us outta here, cryin' or screamin' or mad laughin', you could do 'em all, over and over again, and that door'd still open, sooner or later, one of us or both, it's goin' to open.

PETER

Soon?

ALEX

Soon? How the hell am I supposed to know, do I look like an almanac?
(pauses)
I am sorry I lost my temper.

Peter smiles. Alex stares at him. The sound of a door opening, shutting; then the close crack of gunfire. The lights dim.

When they come up again, the gunfire fades slowly. Peter and Alex have tin plates with food on them, and cups of water. Peter is ravenously eating his, Alex is not.

PETER

What happens if you duck?

ALEX

They let you go. It's a rule.

Peter's eyes open wide, then he realizes he's being kidded.

One guy'll train on your forehead, another'll take your heart—maybe two on your heart, somebody'll take your guts, even got a guy on your kneecaps. They don't take to duckin'.

PETER

You're not eating.

ALEX

Don't I know that? "You're not eating."
(laughs)
I'm worried about my figure. Nothin' but water and starch could blow a man into a skin balloon.

Be an easy target then, wouldn't I, course they'd have to hold my string else I'd just float away outta range.

Big skin balloon in the sky.

Be a cheap way to travel, floatin' across the country.

I could see it all. If the weather was good. Maybe I'd take your tongue along with me.

> *Pause. Alex raises his plate.*

You can finish this—

> *Peter rises to get it.*

Slop!

> *Peter collects it, takes it back to his cot.*

PETER
You might want it later. My mother always said that, "You might—"

ALEX
Your mother some kind of chef?

PETER
Chef? No.

ALEX
I was born minus a mother.

> *Peter stops eating.*

                        PETER

How's that possible?

                        ALEX
                       (smiles)

I was a born killer.

> *Peter laughs nervously. Silence. The tin plate drops from his lap to the ground.*

                        PETER

Dammit! Dammit, they could give us trays, trays or handles to hold onto this—slop!

> *He slams the other plate to the ground.*

                        ALEX
               (moving around the room)

I am still alive, Rebecca. I think I am still alive. Every day I am more alive than the day before. They keep not coming.

I know you're alive, you and Ruth. Jamie found a way.

This little fool eats, he eats at my stomach! I play with him but he is a raw ulcer on my stomach, he is feasting on me!

But I stay sane, I will not die mad, Rebecca.

I can still taste you. I have not lost your taste.

> *The lights dim, then come up low, night.*

Peter gets off his bed, watches Alex to be sure he is asleep and then turns over his mattress. He goes back to sleep. The lights come up.

      PETER
     (laughing)

And?

      ALEX
    (smiling broadly)

And—that's the end.

      PETER

No!

      ALEX

The rest I leave to your imagination.

      PETER

My imagination? You invented it? You made it up?

      ALEX
     (smiles)

You make one up.

      PETER
   (long pause as he thinks)

I can't.

ALEX
(slightly touched and amused)
Never?

PETER
Almost! Twice.

Alex laughs. The sound of a door opening, shutting; then the close crack of gunfire.

ALEX
(speaking rapidly, not directly at Peter)
I am in love with a girl named Rebecca, her hair is the color of oak tree bark and her eyes are green like the leaves. She is five years younger than I am but I have loved her since she was only eleven. I have loved her forever, I suppose—

PETER
Is—is she—

ALEX
She is with my brother Jamie, and my sister, my sister Ruth. They have been together since the night—since the night they ran away. They escaped and they are safe now, they are safe somewhere together. I know that.

Her eyes are green like the leaves and we have made love together, near the pond, we have made love together near the pond in the daytime and at night.

PETER

My sister's name is June, she—

ALEX

Your sister! Fuck your sister! Do you think I care about your goddam sister? Your hairy worm of a sister!

> *Peter jumps at Alex, then wrestles him to the floor. After a few moments of struggling, Alex, on the bottom, laughs softly. Peter sits up and looks at him. Silence.*

PETER

What's the joke?

ALEX

We are the joke. You and me. Twisting brains on this cold-scum floor of a room, we twist on this floor and try to break arms and faces and we might be dead in five minutes—six slices of steel wedged into us into the holes, filling the holes!

That, Peter my friend, is the joke ...

PETER

It's not—

ALEX

And the joke is almost ...

PETER

It's not my—

ALEX
It has been almost over for a week and . . .

PETER
It's not my idea—

ALEX
It will continue to be . . .

PETER
It's not my idea of—

ALEX
Almost over.

PETER
It's not my idea of a joke! I'm more scared than you, that's why.

ALEX
There a tool for measurin' scaredness?

Peter touches his lower stomach.

ALEX
(laughs)
You got the runs?

Peter nods.

ALEX
Intestinal victories don't count.

PETER

What counts?

ALEX

Bad luck.

PETER

What about—God?

ALEX

Who?

PETER

God.

ALEX

Oh, God.

Pray? Go ahead. You don't stand losin' much.

> *Peter thinks for a moment, then gets down on his knees, looks around for the best angle and finally decides to pray up to the window. He is about to begin when he notices that Alex has not moved. He looks at him. Alex shakes his head. Peter beckons him.*

ALEX

You pray. I'll listen.

PETER
(prepares himself)
God, Dear God!

He looks at Alex.

ALEX
That's a good start. Go on.

PETER
Dear God, we're—I—I'm speaking to you from this cell where we-I've been for a week now, waiting. I'm not much good at praying, I mean I've never done it so—so formal before, I hope that doesn't matter to you. It's not supposed to. God, I need your help. I've done nothing wrong, if I did I wouldn't pray like this, it's just that-that I don't want to die right now. There's no one else who'll be praying for me, so I thought—we thought it wouldn't hurt any.

Please help us God! They've kept us waiting so long! I can't take it, Lord. I can't take it any longer!!
(tries to regain control)
I'm sorry, I told you I wasn't good at it.
(formally, as if this is the prayer)
Dear God, please help me now and I will never stop praying to you.
(pause)
And please help Alex, who is here with me, and who is my friend. Amen. Amen!

Alex grabs the pillow from Peter's bed. Peter gets up and walks to his cot, where he lies down. The lights fade and then come up dimly.

Peter takes the pillow out of Alex's sleeping hands and goes back to his cot. The lights dim out and come up again.

Alex is on his cot. Peter is flipping the mattress again.

ALEX
"Nothing I can control. Just a habit."

Sounds like a—fixation to me. Normal and out of control.

Not a man in this world has to piss exactly when he gets outta bed.

It's all in your nut.
(touches his head)
Uncle of mine didn't piss four days straight. That's a fact.

Regular habits he had, too. Said his stomach ached an unbearable lot, carried him to the hospital, doctor asked when's the last time he pissed. Uncle sat straight, opened his eyes wide, "Goddam it doc," he said, "I just knowed I forgot somthin'..." Then he opened up all over the bed. Distant uncle he was.

Peter is silent, Alex looks at him.

How come you didn't laugh?

PETER
(as if he's thought of a story)
Alex, I've got a confession.

ALEX
(calling)
Priest!

PETER
No! Not that kind.

ALEX
What's another kind?

PETER
It's about my mother.

ALEX
The chef?

PETER
I lied to you. She's dead.

ALEX
(matter of fact)
Your mother's dead?

PETER
She died three years ago, after June.

ALEX

After June?

PETER

June. My sister.

(silence)

ALEX
(forcing himself to say it)

I am sorry.

Alex turns over on his bed. Peter shrugs. Silence.

PETER

Will you tell me about him, about your father? Something.

Alex looks up sharply.

ALEX
(after a moment)

He had—his hands had blue thick veins, braided around each knuckle, enormous hands, stronger than any man I know, because he worked in his rose garden every day.
(Pause.)
And that's about my father.

PETER

On what?

ALEX

Roses.

(to himself rather than to Peter)
He used to tell us when we were little that if we ran into the rose garden, if we hurt the roses we'd only be hurtin' ourselves, 'cause roses, even the frailest roses, they are things of beauty—

PETER

That's true, that's—

ALEX
(with disgust)
... as beautiful as any breathtaking creature, and twice as helpless. He never sold any and he never picked any. Every autumn he would fold the dead roses back into the earth, he said it was the only place roses belonged, that they were too terribly beautiful to be anywhere else.
(pause)
He was foldin' roses the day they came.

They could've asked! We would've given 'em what they wanted, if they had asked. War or no war, a family's got its roots.

Deracinate's what it was! I saw them through the kitchen window, Jamie was makin' one of his special faces for the girls, and they were gigglin' behind me, gigglin' when they strode into the garden and began pullin' father towards the house!

Jamie knew the way—they didn't realize that—I just pushed 'em through the door, if I hadn't looked out that window—I just told 'em to run! run to the woods, keep runnin'!

(pause)
Father sat in the captain's chair, him, the one without an ear guarded over us while the others searched the house. The muscle in my father's jaw bulged in and out as he heard them runnin' through the rooms upstairs! I rubbed his shoulders, "Don't worry, father, they're in the woods by now, the woods!" I whispered. I heard a gun cock! I looked up and then he shot my father. He shot my father in the head. He thought we was plannin' to jump on him and while I was rubbin' my father's shoulders he shot a bullet through my father's eye.

> *The sound of a door opening, shutting: then the close crack of gunfire. Peter looks up. Alex seem not to hear it. Alex continues.*

They pinned me onto the floor, and then I—I slobbered. They laughed. He laughed, the one without the ear, a high, skinny laugh. Then they let me take him outside, I wouldn't let them help! I won't cry again, I promised you I won't cry again.
(pause)
They reached inside and pulled his heart out. Pulled his heart like a deep-root weed! War or no war, they could've asked!

Jamie took 'em, they made it okay, Jamie knows the country well as any of us—
(laughs)
—the little bastard. Jamie could get 'em through a whole goddam army!

Jamie this, Jamie that!

(angry)

Makin' me wait. I'll wait, I've got a eye for faces, photographic, that's what it is, photographic, they just might as well needled that face through my eyeball, right smack in.

(begins to mumble)

I am in love with a girl named Rebecca, her hair is the color of oak tree bark and her eyes are green like the leaves; we have made love—

Peter reaches up and touches his leg gently.

Keep away from me! Don't touch my shoulders!

(low)

Don't come near me again, you make me puke.

PETER

Alex?

ALEX

I hate to look at you!

Friends.

(laughs, continues to laugh)

I despise you. I despise you!

Alex laughs. Peter begins to laugh, too.

PETER

(laughing)

I don't care.

ALEX

What?

PETER
(laughing)

I don't care.

The bolt on the door is opened. The door swings out.

VOICE

Which one's Cable?

Alex moves towards the door, but as he does so Peter jumps up, laughing, pushes him out of the way.

PETER

That's me. I'm Cable.

He exits. Alex rushes to the door which slams in his face. He beats on the door. Alex stands for a moment, goes to Peter's cot, takes the pillow and returns to his own cot. The lights fade out. Music comes up.

THE END

MINE

A Play by David Epstein

MINE

was produced by the Actors' Theatre of Louisville in November 1982. It was directed by Frazier W. Marsh and featured the following cast:

Rita-Jean Morgan	Mary Diveny
Bonnie Morgan	Kerstin Kilgo
Lynda Butcher	Dawn Didawick
Patti-Faye Howard	Nancy Mette
Frank Morgan	Vaughn McBride
Men	William Mesnik, Murphy Guyer

"Black Lung" by Hazel Dickens.

MINE

The houselights are up. Four men, their backs to us, mostly, prepare themselves for another day in the mine. They are in various stages of pulling on their work gear and dropping their home clothes into wire baskets strung from the ceiling on pulleys. The baskets hover over each man's bench. When they are loaded with clothes, the miners tug at the rusty chains, raising their baskets high up where they stay in full view, swaying easily.

The room is grimy and spare: benches, a row of sinks against one wall, and a mirror above them. There's a coal stove, up right, vented out the back wall and two buckets of coal beside it. One of the men throws in a fresh scoop, disturbing the embers. The windows have no curtains and what we see is one more gray winter day. There's a front door, down right, and a back door, up left.

A steam whistle blows from outside. The last basket is pulled up to join the others swaying above, and the men, finally outfitted for a day of work, leave the ready-room.

The houselights go to half and then down.

The lights come up low.

We hear the clatter of carriers taking the men into the mountain. Gradually, the clatter fades. Outside are the movements of light-machinery and one or two voices pitched above the sounds giving a quick direction, calling a name: the usual morning sounds at the mine.

After a few beats, there is a sudden, violent roar from the mountain. It rocks the room and is followed by a second thunderous and shattering tremor. The baskets begin to swing wildly, a coal pail falls over, spilling chunks of coal to the floor.

The door of the stove swings open and the redness burns out at us.

A moment's silence, then a shrill, piping alarm begins to blow over and over. We hear the staccato shouts of frightened men: "Number Two! Number Two!" and the disruptive sounds of unplanned action and panic.

Someone rushes through the ready room full-tilt and out the rear door. The alarm keeps sounding above the commotion.

The lights slowly drop to black. When they bump back up full, the alarm has ceased screaming.

Ambulance sirens climb toward the mine. The voices and sounds outside are urgent but controlled. The baskets have steadied.

In the doorway, a scarf over her head, snow on the shoulders of her dark cloth coat, is RITA-JEAN MORGAN. She is tall, gaunt and leathery. Fifty years old, she could be seventy or forty; it's hard to tell. She stands still a moment, taking in the room.

She notices the spilled coal and the open stove and moves toward them. She bends down to shovel the coal back into the bucket with a scoop. She tosses some of it into the fire shuts the stove with the edge of the scoop, the way she's done it all her life, and drops the scoop back into the bucket.

As she's finishing, a young woman rushes quickly into the room, all movement and agitation.

BONNIE MORGAN is wearing a blue parka, her blond hair wet with snow. She's sixteen. She moves towards Rita-Jean, who stands up, stopping Bonnie short.

> RITA-JEAN

Nothin'?

> BONNIE
> (excited)

Teevee's got it.

She follows Rita-Jean back to the benches. Rita-Jean looks overhead, spots something familiar in a basket and takes the bench below it. Bonnie sits on one next to her, pulls off her jacket, shakes out her hair, keeping an eye on the older woman the whole time. She's jumpy and ill at ease.

The siren gets louder and then stops as the ambulance arrives. Rita-Jean has removed her scarf and lights a cigarette.

                    BONNIE
They're bringin' ambulances and all—

Rita-Jean nods, smokes.

                    BONNIE
How do they know who all's in there? For certain.

                    RITA-JEAN
                (not looking at her)
They got a list.

                    BONNIE
Suppose they got it wrong?

                    RITA-JEAN
They're good at lists.

                    BONNIE
Nobody's perfect.

                    RITA-JEAN
                (turns to her)
You see Steven and his daddy out there with the rest of 'em?

Bonnie shakes her head No. Rita-Jean nods. A silence.

                    BONNIE
I could feel it all the way down at Fisher's. The whole ground atremble.

She takes in the room for the first time. Rita-Jean stares dead ahead.

                    BONNIE
                  (shakes her head)
This is weird bein' in here.
                    (fidgets)
We could wait outside.

Rita-Jean says nothing. Bonnie discovers the baskets overhead, is about to mention them but thinks better of it.

The door opens.

LYNDA BUTCHER comes in, leaving the door open behind her. She's thirty, and once, too long ago, she was a beautiful girl. She has a quick eye and a sharp, intelligent face.

Rita-Jean looks up at her as she enters.

                    LYNDA
Nothin'.

Rita-Jean nods. PATTI-FAYE HOWARD hesitates outside the door, unable to come in.

                    LYNDA
                  (impatient)
Come in, Patti-Faye—

She comes in and closes the door quietly. She's in her early twenties and looks like a pudgy child who's been scolded too many times.

PATTI-FAYE
(softly)
Nothin'—

Lynda looks up as she takes off her hat and picks out the right basket. She moves to sit under it, only to find Bonnie already there. She stands over the bench and Bonnie gets the idea and shuffles to the next one. Lynda sits down.

After Patti-Faye has removed her scarf (she does everything slowly), she looks up and locates her man's basket, under which Bonnie is now seated.

PATTI-FAYE
'Scuse me, Bonnie.

Bonnie, annoyed by the whole thing, moves to the fourth bench. She looks up and notices her man's clothes and is about to point it out when everything clicks and she remains quiet.

From outside comes the sound of another ambulance arriving and cars and trucks pulling up.

PATTI-FAYE
How far would they be, Mrs. Morgan?

RITA-JEAN
On the way in, best I can tell.

LYNDA
Dust then. If they weren't shootin' the solid—

RITA-JEAN
Could be dust. Could be the mountain just give out.

BONNIE
Steven says they check that. I asked him how dangerous was it, and he says the company's supposed to check it by law. It's scary he says, but he likes things a touch scary!

LYNDA
The only thing they check are the books.

A silence as they sit on their benches.

LYNDA
This place don't get any prettier, Rita-Jean.

Rita-Jean snorts in agreement.

PATTI-FAYE
Jack says they paint it now and again.

LYNDA
(she doesn't believe a word Jack says)
Does he?

> BONNIE

I wonder do they sweep it now and again?

> LYNDA
> *(with a look)*

They sweep it every time they paint it.

Bonnie laughs. Rita-Jean snorts.

> PATTI-FAYE
> *(matter of fact)*

Well, that's what he says.

> LYNDA
> *(pause)*

You'd be one whole lot better off not takin' everything Jack Howard states as gospel.

> PATTI-FAYE

He's my husband, ain't he?

Lynda nods slowly.

> BONNIE

It smells in here—

> PATTI-FAYE
> *(to Lynda)*

There's just no call to get personal, that's all.

LYNDA

What do you want to discuss, Patti-Faye, the Pepsi test? The fact that we're up here is personal, ain't it? This ain't *practice*, you know. This here is as personal as you can get!

PATTI-FAYE
(sullen)

That's not what I meant.

BONNIE

It smells like when you take off your shoes.

> *Bonnie lights a cigarette, holds up the pack, but there are no takers.*
>
> *Rita-Jean gets to her feet, starts for the front door. There's a knock on it before she gets there. The women focus. Rita-Jean opens the door. We can't see who she's talking to and the voices are too low to hear.*
>
> *When she turns around, she's carrying four styrofoam cups on a wooden shingle. The door closes behind her.*

RITA-JEAN
(approaching with the coffee, shakes her head)

Nothin'.

> *They sit easier, taking the coffee from her and thanking her. Rita-Jean sits back down. They sip from the cups, quiet a moment.*

                    BONNIE
I can't stand sugar in a cup of coffee.

                    PATTI-FAYE
There's no sugar *in* this coffee.

    Bonnie looks at her.

                    BONNIE
It's sweet, ain't it?

                    PATTI-FAYE
Not to me it's not.

    Bonnie looks to Lynda and Rita-Jean, but they are not responding.

                    BONNIE
You wanna switch?

                    PATTI-FAYE
No. I don't take sugar.

                    BONNIE
You just said there weren't any sugar in it!

                    PATTI-FAYE
That's why I'm keepin' it.

                    BONNIE
Well if that don't beat all—I'm tryin' to tell you—

                    RITA-JEAN
                  (cutting her off)
It's just poor coffee, that's all.

    Bonnie and Patti-Faye exchange a look, say nothing.

                      LYNDA
                    (sipping)
It's yesterday's—

                    PATTI-FAYE
Amen.

                      LYNDA
Brewed straight through the hind-end of a mule.

    Bonnie, sipping, laughs and coughs.

                    RITA-JEAN
                    (factual)
He said there's more where that come from.

                      LYNDA
                     (harsh)
Ain't they generous with their coffee!

    A silence.

    Patti-Faye starts crying, quietly. She gets up and moves slowly towards the front door. Exits.

LYNDA

I don't know why she's cryin'—

Bonnie looks at her.

LYNDA

She might just get fortunate.

BONNIE

Fortunate?

LYNDA
(to Rita-Jean)

That girl's got marks across her butt looks like a waffle iron! And that's just to begin with.

Bonnie is listening. Rita-Jean nods.

LYNDA
(with disgust)

Him chasin' up and down the holler like he does—old pickled rooster got no business with that girl.

She shakes her head, loses her anger and disgust, cradles her head in her hands, then to herself, softly:

Oh Herman Butcher, if you come out, I know you're just gonna go back in there again, damn fool of a man—

Patti-Faye returns, closing the door behind her. They all look up.

PATTI-FAYE
(embarrassed to have everyone looking at her)
Nothin' yet. But close. They're sayin'.

She comes to her bench and sits down.

PATTI-FAYE
Rainin' now.

Lynda's head turns listening for the rain, an anxious look on her face.

PATTI-FAYE
You know over Buffalo Creek it rained for days and days just before. All that rain melted out the dam and then the black water came roarin' down the holler like a train—
(pause)
My cousin Lou-Ann lived over there.
(pause)
She moved to Charleston, but now every night it rains she still goes to bed dressed, with her shoes on, just in case.
(pause)
They never did find that boy of hers—Wesley-Lee.
(pause)
He was overweight.

Bonnie gets up, restless. She walks upstage to the stove, opens it, throws more coal inside, slams it closed too hard. She stands by it, her arms hugging her sides. A silence.

                            BONNIE
You know they're showin' goose-down in all the magazines.

            Softly, to herself, Patti-Faye has begun to hum as Bonnie
            is speaking.

                            BONNIE
                         (daydreaming)
Overcoats warm as toast, light as a feather. All you need under 'em is one thin layer. Stay warm and fashionable all day long—

                            LYNDA
It's like wearin' pillows. Everybody puts 'em on looks seven months pregnant. What it is, is bad fashion.

            The humming quietly becomes a song. Patti-Faye has an
            astonishing, clear and bell-like voice.

                          PATTI-FAYE
"The mines was his first love, but never his friend . . . "

            Gradually, almost under their breath, the other women
            join in. First Bonnie, then Rita-Jean, but not Lynda. She
            can't bear the song.

                          ALL THREE
"He went to the bossman but he closed the door.
It seems you're not wanted when you're sick and you're poor."

They take it through all together, conscious of their unity and the momentary comfort it brings them, never looking at one another.

When it's over, they are quiet a moment, still caught in the web; maybe someone hums a chorus, then—

                RITA-JEAN
     (almost a reverie, slowly savoring the names)
Craynor, Phelps, Topmost—
           (shakes her head in sadness)

                 LYNDA
                 (nods)
Phyllis.

                RITA-JEAN
                 (nods)
Phyllis.

                PATTI-FAYE
Buffalo Creek.

           LYNDA / RITA-JEAN
Buffalo Creek.

                 BONNIE
Saunders?

      RITA-JEAN / LYNDA / PATTI-FAYE
Pardee.

                    BONNIE
Dutch Creek?

                    LYNDA
Dutch Creek.

                    RITA-JEAN
                    (pause, quietly)
Hyden.

                    LYNDA/PATTI-FAYE
                    (nod)
Hyden.

                    BONNIE
Farmington!

                    RITA-JEAN/LYNDA
Farmington.

                    PATTI-FAYE / BONNIE
                    (simultaneously)
Hurricane Creek.

       They look at one another. A silence.

                    LYNDA
                    (with finality)
Centrailia.

RITA-JEAN
(low, almost a whisper)

Centrailia! Centrailia—

(shakes her head)

A silence.

PATTI-FAYE
(a strangulated outburst)

Every time they call it an act of God! Then they go and do it again. God don't go around blowin' up mineshafts; it's not His way. Company can say what they please. They just keep skinnin' us and goin' about their business, skinnin' us alive, skinnin' us dead, and blamin' God Almighty. It ain't right.

LYNDA

They ain't in it alone, Patti-Faye.

BONNIE

Who says?

LYNDA
(cool)

The government lets 'em kill us 'cause it's big business, and we let 'em kill us 'cause it's the only business. The company don't do it by themself. The government gives 'em the permit—they just go ahead and let us get hurt 'cause it's a whole lot cheaper'n followin' regulations. But they couldn't do it if we didn't work for 'em, could they?

Rita-Jean snorts.

                        PATTI-FAYE
Amen.

    Bonnie's thinking it over.

                        BONNIE
There *is* nothin' else.

                        LYNDA
There is a whole world outside this valley, I know you've seen the ads for it.

    Bonnie looks at her sharply.

                        LYNDA
We all just seem to have trouble gettin' over there.
    (pause)
I mightta gone myself once, but I fell in love with Herman Butcher when I was sixteen, and determined.

                        BONNIE
    (with a look at Rita-Jean)
Purvis went.

                        LYNDA
Purvis did.

                        BONNIE
    (low, with a glance at Rita-Jean)
She begged him. She talked at him and talked at him, told him how she didn't want another Morgan man in the mines if she could help it, and how smart he was and fulla—possibilities. I

heard 'em downstairs, everybody else deep asleep but me listenin' and the two of them whisperin'—
(pause)
She coaxed him along but Purvis, you know was a little nervous. Steven ain't like that. But finally he did pick up, said he'd try six months, see what he could find.
(keeps checking Rita-Jean)
Now all she worries about is him gettin' in bad down there. She sent him away and now she pines for him.

LYNDA

Well—you lose 'em if they stay and you lose 'em if they go—
(stands)
You just lose ' em worse around here.
(goes to the front door and exits)

BONNIE

She does have a bitter streak, don't she?

The others say nothing. Bonnie circles the benches, pacing, anxious with energy.

BONNIE
(as she moves)
I don't know why we have to stay in here. Everybody else is outside! Sheriffs and deputies and doctors, just about every miner in the whole holler—
(looks out a window)
That's a television camera!

She rushes for the door. Patti-Faye starts up.

RITA-JEAN

Bonnie Morgan.

Bonnie stops. Patti-Faye sits back down, fast.

BONNIE

Well I wanna see what's goin' on!

RITA-JEAN
(hard)

What's goin' on is they are diggin' in that shaft for Steven and his daddy and Jack Howard and Herman Butcher! Nothin' else is *goin'* on.

BONNIE
(longingly)

But it's television—

RITA-JEAN

It's a liar. Don't you know that?

PATTI-FAYE

Amen.

Bonnie turns her back and goes to the window.

Lynda, excited, cold, enters quickly carrying more coffee, talking as she does.

LYNDA

They got voices! They don't know who and they don't know how many. But voices.

She shuts the door, brings the coffee over. The news turns up the tension.

LYNDA

It's a damn circus out there!

She heads for the stove to warm herself. Bonnie turns back to the window, looks out.

PATTI-FAYE

How far off are they, Lynda?

LYNDA
(sipping)

Close

BONNIE
(frustrated)

This is about the dirtiest window in the state of West Virginia!

RITA-JEAN

Don't be peerin'.

Bonnie stays at the window, a moment's defiance, then turns away.

LYNDA
(angry)
Every time somethin' loud happens around here we get discovered by America again. You should see 'em with their cameras and microphones interviewin' Hally Jessup. Hally Jessup of all! Blind in one eye and a twitch in the other. I suppose he looks real *country* to 'em—

PATTI-FAYE
I thought he was half-blind in both?

BONNIE
They say a blue shirt shows best on teevee.

RITA-JEAN
Voices or a voice, Lynda?

The question focuses their attention.

LYNDA
I can't say, Rita-Jean. Nobody's certain yet.

Rita-Jean nods.

A silence.

PATTI-FAYE
(quietly)
When they pulled my daddy out the last time, he was so twisted up he wouldda been better off dead.

Bonnie looks up, a shiver crawls her spine.

PATTI-FAYE
He had always been such a big man—
> *(her voice trails off)*

Silence.

Outside a jackhammer starts up, adding to the hum. After a moment:

LYNDA
> *(to herself)*

Herman Butcher was the finest athlete in Logan County, West Virginia. And the handsomest boy, too. He had muscles like a marble statue when I first saw him and his body was true and straight! with just a little curly black hair, right here, on his chest. And he could wrestle! Nobody could out-wrestle Herman Butcher.
> *(pause)*

Every girl from Logan to Saunders had a sweet tooth for him.
> *(remembering, defiant)*

But he couldn't see nobody but me.
> *(pause)*

He used to push his daddy's pickup out the driveway at two a.m. and jump it goin' down the hill. Then he'd shut it off and coast right to outside our house. He always carried a ladder with him and he'd bring it under my window and we'd go ridin'.
> *(pause)*

Once we came back home at six in the mornin' and there was no ladder standin' there. Nobody ever spoke a word of it, either.

(pause)
On the day we got married my daddy went out and bought ten red and blue ribbons, the kind with long tails on 'em. He presented that old ladder to Herman tied up as a gift! He liked Herman.
(pause)
You know sometimes he coughs so hard in his sleep now I have to grab onto him or he'll roll off the bed.
(pause)
And his legs seize up. I gotta rub the knots outta them so they don't cramp on him in the middle of the night. He's bruised over like an old apple, but those hairs on his chest are still black!
(Pause)
And his body's still all marbly.
(pause, bitter)
It just ain't straight anymore.
(after a moment)
I wonder what the hell he sees now when he looks at me?

A silence.

BONNIE
(low, fiercely)
Steven's comin' outta that mine in one piece.

She goes for the door.

RITA-JEAN
Bonnie—

BONNIE
(a little smile)
Don't worry. I ain't gonna embarrass nobody.

She exits.

PATTI-FAYE
Who's watchin' that little boy of hers?

They don't respond.

PATTI-FAYE
Most likely Joyce-Ann next door. Or maybe her mama come up.
(pause)
I heard Joyce-Ann and him bought an RCA unit so big they had to tear off the front door to get it inside.
(pause)
Forty-eight inches!

Lynda shoots her a glance. She nods.

A silence. The jackhammer pounds outside.

PATTI-FAYE
My kids are over Gutheries'.
(pause)
Forty-eight inches, imagine that.

LYNDA
(with an edge)
How many televisions has Jack Howard got you, Patti-Faye?

PATTI-FAYE
(thinks)
Four. Workin'—twenty-one inch is the biggest though—color.

LYNDA
What the hell difference is watchin' a forty-eight inch television gonna make when he goes out on you and you're sittin' there alone with three babies upstairs?

PATTI-FAYE
(sharply)
It'd help.

LYNDA
I'll tell you what'd help, Patti-Faye—

PATTI-FAYE
God hears everythin' you're thinkin'.

LYNDA
And He's agreein' with me, too.

Rita-Jean suddenly stands up.

They stop talking and listen. The sounds outside have changed. The jackhammer has stopped pounding. They listen hard. It's silent.

Bonnie bursts into the room, her hair and face wet with rain.

                    BONNIE
                 (out of breath)
Patti-Faye! They're bringin' out Jack Howard. He's okay! They say he's beat up some but he's okay. They got an ambulance goin'—

For a moment Patti-Faye and Lynda catch one another's eye. Something passes between them, unspoken.

Patti-Faye, without a word, reaches up and quickly pulls the chains, bringing her man's basket rattling down to her. She empties his clothes.

Lynda and Bonnie watch her. Rita-Jean sits back down.

Patti-Faye bundles the clothes into her arms.

                  PATTI-FAYE
              (hesitate, ambivalent)
Oh God—

She looks around at the others, and then heads for the door as fast as she can without running. She exits.

                    BONNIE
                   (excited)
There's other voices too—

                  RITA-JEAN
              (not looking at her)
Other voices, or a voice?

                        BONNIE
Other voices!

    Rita-Jean nods.

                        BONNIE
            (moving nervously around the room)
They got the cameras goin', they got stretchers all lined up. Everybody let out such a whoop! Did you hear it?
                        (pause)
I didn't wait on seein' him. Just as soon as word came out I ran right back here.
                    (pause, a realization)
She didn't do nothin', did she? I mean Patti-Faye. She didn't say nothin'—no whoop, no holler or nothin'—

    She looks at the other two, but they are not paying her any attention.

    Silence.

    A muffled cheer pierces their stillness, electrifying them.

    They stare at the door.

    Patti-Faye throws it open and leans inside.

                      PATTI-FAYE
                        (huffing)
Lynda!

(she grins, nods quickly and beckons her)

Lynda leaps to her feet.

LYNDA
(short and triumphant)

Herman!

She starts to rush out, stops. She turns around and drops to her knees in front of Rita-Jean, hugs her and holds her. Rita-Jean pats her gently.

Bonnie lowers Lynda's basket for her. Lynda gets up and gathers her man's clothes with a thank-you nod to Bonnie, unable to speak.

Bonnie goes right to her and hugs Lynda, whose arms are filled with clothes.

Lynda hurries out the door without looking back.

Bonnie moves after her and closes the door. She turns around and moves back into the room, slowly.

Rita-Jean looks up and she and Bonnie find themselves staring at one another for a long moment. The look might be a distant embrace.

Outside an ambulance starts up; a siren begins to sound and it moves down the mountainside.

Bonnie goes to the window, peers outside.

Rita-Jean walks to the stove, opens it and shovels in another scoop-full. Stands warming herself.

BONNIE
(looking out as the siren fades)
Steven figures if he can work steady the next six months to a year we'll be able to move into a place—

Rita-Jean looks over at her, says nothing, goes back to the bench and lights a cigarette.

BONNIE
(suddenly anguished, turns to her)
How many times have you been here like this. How many in all these years?

Rita-Jean shakes her head. She doesn't remember, or care to.

BONNIE
(a plea)
Well, I can't pass my life drivin' this mountain and sittin' in this room! It's not for me. I won't do it! I can't—
(shakes her head)
I refuse.

They look at one another. Bonnie turns back to the window abruptly.

A silence.

BONNIE
(uneasy)
Somebody's comin'.

Rita-Jean looks up, brushes her hands off, and walks directly to the door. Bonnie stands still, watching her.

We can't see who's at the door. Then she opens it, and we can only make out hushed tones. After a few moments the door closes. Rita-Jean hesitates at the closed door, gathers herself and turns.

It seems as if a sudden weariness has just taken hold, replacing the tension.

Bonnie is fixed on her as she moves to the sink, rolls up her sleeves, and begins washing her hands, not looking at Bonnie.

Bonnie darts out the door.

Rita-Jean finds a bucket under the sink with a sponge in it and she cleans them out under the tap.

Just as she's finishing, the door opens and TWO MINERS enter carrying a stretcher with A MAN face up, lying in it. He's covered over with a greasy, muddy blanket, and it's clear from the way he is lying that he's dead.

The two miners hesitate, not sure where to set the stretcher down.

Rita-Jean has turned, and for a moment she says nothing, gazing at the covered body.

She motions them to put it across two benches, the head facing upstage, which they do. They stand off, awkwardly. Rita-Jean nods at them, and they back away, turn and exit.

She goes to the body, hesitates, lifts the blanket, looks at the face a moment, satisfies herself and recovers it. She turns away to the sink, as Bonnie rushes back into the room.

She stops, gaping at the body.

Rita-Jean begins to fill the bucket with water.

Bonnie can't take her eyes off the body, trapped by the sight of it.

She doesn't move, breathing hard.

                    RITA-JEAN
                    (not harshly)
Bonnie.

The girl looks at her, frightened.

RITA-JEAN

This mountain don't want but one Morgan today. I can feel it. You hear?

Bonnie nods.

RITA-JEAN
(gently)

Go ahead now. You go be there.

Bonnie doesn't move. Rita-Jean nods at the stricken girl. Bonnie throws herself into Rita-Jean's arms with a sob. They embrace. Rita-Jean eases her away, patting her.

Bonnies rises uneasily, and then runs for the door.

Rita-Jean watches her go. Her eyes seem to hang on the door before she turns back to her man. She looks at him a long moment, finishes filling the bucket and carries it towards the body, taking the sponge and the bar of soap.

RITA-JEAN
(as she approaches)

Here's a man fulla surprises.
(pause)
I always knew *how*; I just never knew when.
(pause)
He taught me to dance the waltz with him so sweet. You won't dance with me again.

(pause)
They wanted to carry you down to the funeral parlor there and clean you up.
(looks at him)
I watched you go down. I watched you skinny-out and go pale. I watched you cripple-up and get busted—
(stops, a fury)
Nobody is gonna clean you up but me!
(silent a moment, shakes her head, looks at him)
You couldda stopped. You had doctor's letters; you had benefits comin'—Oh no, somebody's gotta drive that shuttle. Somebody's gotta run them jaws and work the face. Somebody's gotta lay dynamite and set the timbers, bolt the roof and drill and cut! Somebody's gotta check the belts and run supplies and you *know* somebody's gotta be foreman!
(rinses her sponge, ironic)
It sure beats sittin' at home, don't it, even if you got yourself a pair of lungs like swiss cheese gone gray.
(looks down, quoting him)
"Once a miner quits minin' what the hell is he?" Well, I'll tell you what he is, Frank Morgan, he's alive! He's a husband, even if he can't waltz around the room like he once could. He's a father even if he's coughin' and wheezin' and huntin' for one good deep breath. He's alive!
(silent, then angry)
What's the history of me? My daddy worked the mines. I grew up. My husband worked the mines. I grew old. My boys work the mines. Now I'm dead. I grow dead!
(pause)
What can we do? Where else can we go? What else do we know? Our bones are buried here. Old Dalton bones, old Morgan bones,

baby bones—my blood's in these hills. We're miners. We're from miners. What else do we know—

> *A pause; she reaches down and folds back the blanket, revealing the man's muddy face*

My daddy died at home. Thirty-two years in the mines and he just ran outta breath!
(pauses; after a moment, tenderly)
Any man who can hold three children on one knee and play harmonica at the same time, I always said that's a man for me—and dance the fiddle so sweet. Dance me! Dance me round the room, two of us round and round.
(shakes her head; raises one of his hands, holds it, examines it)
These nails, all square cut—

> *Slowly, a wail begins deep within her. It grows and builds until it erupts into a howl, spilling out of her, surprising her with its force. After it passes she still has his hand in hers. She looks at it strangely.*
>
> *A distant, muffled cheer penetrates the thin walls of the room.*
>
> *She lays the hand back down on his chest. She rises and pulls the chain on the third basket, lowering it. She looks at it a moment, her hand reaches out and gently touches the flannel shirt lying on top. She returns to the stretcher.*

RITA-JEAN

Well, don't you worry, Steven's comin' out. He's comin' out this time—there'll still be a Morgan in the mines.
(bitterly)
Always a Morgan, all waitin' to go underground—and grow up.
(picks up the sponge, begins to clean his face)
And I'll be the one to tell 'em "Get away." I'll say, "Go on, go on if you can and stay out. Let the others break their bones and black their lungs and burn their hearts out underground, and all our hearts up here."
(pause)
I'll be the one to say it and they'll be the ones to stay—till they're spittin' up black in their handkerchiefs and there's no coal left underground and they've ripped it all off the top like skin!

She scrubs at his face, takes a deep breath and brushes the mud-crusted hair back from his forehead, then she rinses the sponge: her voice takes on a determined, strong tone.

Well, I'm goin' on. I ain't gonna roll over into the ground with you. I got family to look after and grandchildren. I still got things to do—I'm goin' on.
(starts cleaning him again; silence, then:)
Somebody's gonna do some hard shovellin' with the earth froze like it is. That's the trouble with dyin' in winter. It's so tough breakin' ground!

The lights have begun to drop. She stares down at him. Finally she reaches her right hand out towards him. Then, after a moment:

RITA-JEAN
(a prayer)

Dance with me again!

She looks down at him, lays a hand atop his.

As the LIGHTS begin to drop, fiddle music stirs the air.

Enter dancing, a YOUNG WOMAN in a colorful skirt and white blouse, and a YOUNG MAN in newly washed jeans and flannel shirt. They move tentatively at first, shyly smiling at one another in the dimming light. And then, with grace, they dance into darkness as Rita-Jean gazes down at her man.

THE END

DECEIVED BY COLIN POWELL

A play by David Epstein

Lyrics by David Epstein
Music by David Epstein
& Robert Montgomery

The world floats in shadow. Platform levels become lighted playing areas, islands of a fluid stage.

Late autumn, 2004.

In darkness we hear the slap-pat-pat of a soft-shoe routine. Stage left, LIGHT up on THE GUIDE, a slick smoothy in a finely tailored U.S. Army uniform, shiny black boots and wrap-around sunglasses and cap. One hand holds the cap in the air as the other beckons. The soft-shoe ends with a flourish.

SONG: "GIRL ON FIRE"

                     GUIDE
                    (sings)

Step up and serve your country
Exotic landscape, friendly tribes
Total cooperation—a few twists, a few bribes

We'll make a man of you sweetheart,
A man if that's your desire
Grateful nation, open arms
Hey—girl on fire!

We can't lose because we're winners
An' guess who's along for the ride?
My man God enlisted, be right by your side

We'll make a man of you sweetheart,
A man if that's your desire

Grateful nation, open arms
Hey—girl on fire!

Be a mechanic, nurse or techno sniper
And help the dirty strangers,
Kill the dirty strangers

We'll make a man of you sweetheart,
A man if that's your desire
Grateful nation, open arms
Hey—girl on fire!

Now here's a gift for all your loved ones
Tell 'em hold on, clean house, n' pray!
Cause you'll be makin'
Democracy, every fuckin' day

We'll make a man of you sweetheart,
A man if that's your desire
Grateful nation, open arms
Hey—girl on fire!

SONG ENDS

> *He starts dancing again as the LIGHT shifts from him to down left where TERRI MEADE ROSE, mid-forties, and ANDREW ROSE, mid-fifties, are in their sunny Santa Monica breakfast nook, coffee and scones. He's got a newspaper, she's reading a script, red pencil in hand. There's a stationary bike nearby.*

TERRI
(not looking up)
People aren't threatened by this war, they just don't care.

ANDREW
That's exactly the point.

TERRI
There's no draft, no angry college kids. Nobody's scared enough to get off their goddam couch.

ANDREW
There's this woman, this mother of a soldier.

TERRI
And they don't want to get disturbed. They hear "Iraq" and change channels, switch stations, blogs.

ANDREW
She could be the focus of a film.

TERRI
There are no visuals. Nobody's marching, nobody's burning anything.

ANDREW
Listen to me.

TERRI
(puts the script down)
I lost someone in a pointless, stupid war thirty years ago, then I watch it happen all over again. Believe me—

ANDREW
Her son was killed in Baghdad. This woman's son.

TERRI
I should call my father. My sister never calls him.

ANDREW
By a sniper—her son.

TERRI
What? I know about her! You'll be wasting your time. It's a tiny little group of protesters waiting for Bush to drive by in his ten-gallon hat.

ANDREW
No. It's growing, the group is growing fast.

TERRI
You can't make a documentary about frustration.

ANDREW
Resistance is building.

TERRI

(gently)

Please, Andrew, please come up with an idea approaching mainstream just once? Something you can actually raise money on—the "M" word.

ANDREW

(ironic)

You know, I'm bankable now, believe it or not.

TERRI

(smiles)

Sweetheart, you made a wonderful documentary; you deserved your nomination.

ANDREW

(amused by her)

You're going to be surprised.

TERRI

Just—please be realistic. A documentary nomination does not mean you are bankable. Shrek is bankable.

ANDREW

Sam says, from what he hears, I won't have any trouble raising money this time.

TERRI

(looks at him deadpan)

He's your cameraman.

ANDREW
(grins)

He's well-connected.

TERRI

I'm sorry. Can we talk about dinner for Toby tonight, please?

ANDREW
(a beat)

Right. Okay. A reservation where? Where would she like to go? What about—a nice, really popular gay restaurant?
(She looks at him.)
I mean as a kind of—an offering, a statement. That we love her—and it doesn't matter.

TERRI

It does matter.

ANDREW
(firmly)

That we love her no matter what her sexual preference.
(a pause)
Some place she's never been, new, exciting—end of her first semester, birthday, homecoming?

TERRI
(looks up)

Sure. Why not. And we could buy her something butch for Christmas, or a nice Chanukah dildo.

ANDREW
She's a remarkable human being.

TERRI
I know that.

ANDREW
And the fact that she's willing to discuss her sexuality with her parents, be—up front. It's—courageous. And it makes me proud of her.

TERRI
Should we throw her a party? A coming-out party?

ANDREW
That's funny.

TERRI
Thank you. And just for the record? She didn't "discuss." She announced. On the phone, into my ear, a bomb. A unique personal weapon of mass destruction.

He looks at her.

TERRI
What?

ANDREW
You took it personally?

                    TERRI

I take everything personally; I had a mother, remember? I know
how it's done.

> *Carrying an overnight bag over her shoulder, their
> daughter TOBY ROSE crosses in shadow to their light.
> She's an eighteen-year-old dynamo in jeans and sneakers
> who moves with grace. There's a super-capable intelli-
> gence about her that tends to mask her vulnerability.
> Even when she's uncertain of her way in the world, you
> sense that eventually Toby will get herself where she
> needs to go.*
>
> *She enters silently and stands just outside their light a
> moment, taking in her parents as if from across a chasm,
> seeing them anew, sensing, perhaps, that while she feels
> strong and filled with life, they suddenly seem smaller,
> and drained.*
>
> *After a moment Andrew turns, sees her.*

                    ANDREW
                    (rising)
Hey, look who's here!

                    TERRI
                    (thrilled)
Sweetheart!

> *Andrew and Terri converge on their only child with open
> arms, embrace her, words flying on top of words—*

ANDREW & TERRI
You got an early flight—I'm so excited!
We would've been there—
You took a cab? Why didn't you call?
Look at you!
My gorgeous baby—

ANDREW
Do we look really old to you?

TERRI
We don't, do we?

ANDREW
It's okay, you can say it: Mom looks younger.

TOBY
(her voice is tight with tension)
I enlisted. Downtown. From the airport.

ANDREW
(not comprehending)
You enlisted downtown?

TOBY
I enlisted.

TERRI
I don't get it. Is this—are we—YouTube, or something?

                            TOBY

In the army.

                            TERRI

You're in a college.

                            TOBY

Boot camp's in a month. I'm starved. What can I eat?

            A stunned silence.

                            ANDREW

Tobe—what are you—did you enlist?

            She nods, reaches for a scone.

                            TERRI

She's serious. You're serious? The army?
            (She nods again. They look at one another.)
Okay, okay, okay—

                            ANDREW
                        (simultaneously)

Wow—woof—

                            TERRI

She's actually done this.

                            ANDREW

Just—on impulse?

Toby shakes her head, No.

TERRI
(to herself)
Who can we call?

ANDREW
Is—how long has this—

TOBY
Since 9/11, but I was too young, duh—obviously.
(re scone)
You can get nothing like this in Swarthmore, Pennsylvania.

TERRI
And—do you remember, you know I lost a brother in Vietnam.

TOBY
Uncle Gus is my hero, Mom. Uncle Harry, too, and Grampa for World War Two. Serving the country is a family tradition you should be proud of.

TERRI
I should? Your cousin talked like this—this comes from Bobby.

TOBY
He tried to enlist.

ANDREW
(stunned)
He was too tall.

TOBY
(matter-of-fact)
He's doing a kind of alternative service.

TERRI

Outsourcing?

ANDREW
(disbelief)
That's not "alternative service." What he's doing? For a contractor?

TOBY
(shrugs)
Helping the war effort. Call it whatever.

ANDREW

It's larceny.

TOBY

It's a dangerous service to the country.

ANDREW

Those corporations are ripping us off.

TERRI
(slumping)
Andrew, pull the stake out of my heart. Where did this come from? She's away one semester.

TOBY

It's not about you, Mom.

TERRI

I'm going to be sick.

TOBY

This is me, who I am. I'm a patriot. My uncles, my grandfather decided for themselves, and I decided for myself. I've done it.

TERRI

They were drafted.

TOBY
(shrugs)

I've gotta pee.

She exits. They are too shaken to speak.

TERRI
(slowly)

We're going to stop this, Andrew.

ANDREW

She's eighteen.

TERRI

Right away!
(to herself)
How do I do this? Downtown, a U.S. Army recruiting person.

(picks up phone)
I can't believe I'm doing this.

ANDREW

On the phone? Why don't you go down there if you're so sure.

TERRI

On the phone? I'm a phone animal, Andrew. Will you let me handle this?

ANDREW
(re Toby)
I mean, there's something impressive going on.

TERRI

She's a college freshman, making a mistake, Andrew.

ANDREW

Maybe she's got to make her own mistakes, Terri. We can't—

TERRI

Please! Can you refrain from quoting—books, or whatever it is.
(quietly)
Andrew—there could be real consequences to this.

ANDREW

Let's just suppose she wants to serve her country.

TERRI

Oh, god.

ANDREW

Give her the benefit of the doubt.

TERRI

What's that mean, serve her country? In Iraq??

ANDREW

She's a smart, thoughtful girl—

TERRI

It's lunacy!

ANDREW

A lot of people were changed by 9/11.

TERRI

She's not from Iowa. She's a rich, confused L.A. kid. You want to know what this is? It's a perverse response to being spoiled.
(a beat)
It's Bobby! That seven-foot numbskull carrying on about how every slob's entitled to democracy—and you, wanting to liberate the poor Iraqis!

ANDREW

Do you have any respect for beliefs that aren't just like yours? Or is it because she'll embarrass you?

TERRI

Of course it's an embarrassment! And a major mistake. A life-threatening—are you accepting this?

(a beat)

Maybe I should call my brother. She visited him and Magdalena in New York. He wouldn't have encouraged this. I can't imagine he would've.

ANDREW

She visited your father, too.

TERRI

Right. He probably showed her Gus's Vietnam medals. You know, I was really enjoying that scone.

ANDREW

Magdalena's brother Angel is in the army.

TERRI

What were his options?

(a beat)

She's done it again.

ANDREW

Done what again?

TERRI

I'm—going to be sick!

She runs off, passing Toby, who watches her go.

ANDREW

Well. How about some—one of my famous omelettes? French toast?

                           TOBY

Why was she running?

          He mimes barfing.

Really? I'll have an omelette. I don't think I've ever seen Mom run.

                          ANDREW
                      (starts cooking)
We're trying to—this is a shock, Toby. And—we want to understand it.

                           TOBY

It's something I have to do.

                          ANDREW

I want to understand it.

          He waits. She hesitates.

                           TOBY
                    (weighing her words)
It's real. It's positive. It's—a decisive act.
                         (a beat)
And it's something I want to earn.

                          ANDREW

Right. What about school?

                           TOBY

No. I stopped concentrating. I just—stopped, I couldn't study.

(struggling)
Okay. This—I got dumped, okay? By this—jock. Don't ask about it! Then I started thinking. I started—about them. I stayed awake, online—news updates, reading blogs.

ANDREW

Who's "them?"

TOBY

I hardly slept. That's all I did the last three weeks.

ANDREW

Them?

TOBY

What? Kids, soldiers. My age. Not rich. Involved. Over there, doing something authentic. And I'm reading Kant—ersatz!

ANDREW

Are bullets more authentic than books?

TOBY

What? Yes! In this case, yes.

ANDREW

Why? Ideas change the way people think, not muscle.

TOBY

Ideas supported by muscle. You can't hold a book up to a terrorist.

ANDREW

The Koran?

TOBY

Are you making this omelette or not?
(a beat)
I'm sorry. You offered.
(He looks at her.)
I've got to start eating right. Boot camp's supposed to be a real bitch.

ANDREW
(cooks)

You know, Tobe, the army doesn't—gay people have to keep quiet, a low profile.

TOBY

I know that.

Terri returns.

TERRI

Just because you're gay doesn't mean you have to be a soldier.

TOBY
(a beat)

I might not be gay anyway.

TERRI

What? You're not gay? Andrew, she's not gay.

TOBY

I didn't say that! God! Why doesn't she listen?

TERRI

I'm listening, I'm listening. So are you, or aren't you? Which?

They both look at her.

What?

ANDREW

Never heard of bisexuality?

TERRI
(considers)

Okay, I'll take it! So what is this, Private Benjamin? You're going to carry weapons? Jump over—sharp things— "obstacles," crawl under wires, and and climb nets, do things—in mud? Are you a masochist? You'll be a mess in two days, in tears!

TOBY

Maybe you'll be surprised by what I can do.

TERRI

No.
(gently)

I'm never surprised by what you can do. Aside from me, I think you're the most capable person I've ever known.
(a beat)

I happen to be terrified.

(pause)
Andrew, please fix me a drink. I need something strong—a potion.

Toby is looking at her, surprised. LIGHTS SHIFT.

Up Right, soft LIGHT finds TWO SOLDIERS in BOOT CAMP T-shirts and fatigues doing calisthenics.

In SANTA MONICA, Toby begins to pack a bag.

After exercising, the SOLDIERS take a break. One of them, TIM, an eighteen-year-old, has a guitar, strums chords.

Andrew, in shorts with a towel around his neck, rides the stationary bike as Terri hovers around Toby, who is packing.

TERRI
Your Uncle Harry doesn't think it's a good idea either. And he's a veteran.

TOBY
That's because I'm a woman.

TERRI
And I went downtown, I enquired.

TOBY
(calmly, as she packs)
It's out of your hands, Mom.

TERRI

I didn't identify myself. Just—tell them you're gay, and you're—excused.

Toby shoots her a look.

Okay, don't lie, say—bisexual. They understand that. I checked.

Andrew keeps peddling, out of breath.

You can support the war, if that's what you actually believe. Tell her, Andrew.

TOBY

Thank you.

ANDREW
(peddling)

Support it without joining. We'll respect your decision.

TERRI

Even if we disagree with everything you say about it.

ANDREW

I supported it. Initially. A lot of people did.

TERRI
(losing it)

You don't need to do this! You're an achiever. You've always been an achiever—since Pre-K! You turned down the Ivy League! You're on a Phi Beta Kappa track.

(to Andrew)
Would you stop peddling!

TOBY
I finished one semester of college.

ANDREW
(stops peddling)
I was deceived by Colin Powell.

TERRI
Your professors love you! You have untold career opportunities. It's all opening up for you, it's huge, huge potential—it's enormous!

TOBY
Joining the army doesn't limit career potential, except maybe for show business, which I detest.

ANDREW
Sweetheart, if you're considering a political career—

TERRI
Is that supposed to hurt my feelings?

ANDREW
There's living proof you can draft-dodge, lie, get endless deferments...

TOBY
I have no interest in politics.

ANDREW

... and still be elected president of the United States.

TOBY

I want my AIT to be in—maybe in Med as a C4 Corpsman.

TERRI

Could we not talk in acronyms, please.

TOBY

I might want to train as a medic. After Boot. It's the next step.

TERRI

A medic?

ANDREW

Really? Wow. That's—I'm impressed. You can handle—all that? Why are you shaking you head?

TERRI

She barfs! At blood, the sight of blood, since you were six. A cut on your pinky. I'll say no more.

TOBY

Not any longer.

TERRI

Oh? How do you know?

TOBY

I've seen stuff.

ANDREW

What kind of stuff?

TOBY

Cadavers, autopsies. I took an EMT course. Ambulances, lots of blood. I didn't turn away. Okay, I did at first. But—actually I'm—intrigued. I like it. Okay? I can do it. I'm kinda into blood now. A combat medic.

TERRI

This is getting a little weird for me.

ANDREW

Are you sure women can become combat medics?

TOBY

What? I'll find that out. I don't want to be a nurse.

TERRI

Find out how many of them survive.

ANDREW

Terri.

TERRI

What? This is not some— "career choice" she's making, this is— I've lived through this! That's what we're talking about. Face it, Andrew! It's crazy. Come on, she's—she's watching operations with—with stitches, and organs for god's sake! She should be in her dorm looking at Facebook or having sex like everybody else. Go to medical school if you want to help people. Or become a vet!

Toby stands up straight, suitcase in hand, turns from them and exits. Tim's guitar plays her across to BOOT CAMP.

LIGHTS keep Terri and Andrew alive.

In BOOT CAMP, Stage Right, are the Two Soldiers, JOJO, a young woman, and TIM. Toby approaches with her suitcase.

The GUIDE, now wearing red clown bloomers, a fatigue jacket, and cap, soft-shoes into the light. As he speaks, Toby opens her suitcase, begins changing into a T-shirt and fatigues.

GUIDE

Welcome, CottageCheeseAss! And prepare for sandbox heaven. Do you speak the language? No? Have you heard the one about the CottageCheeseAss who says to the sergeant, "What do I need to know?"

He does a little dance step as others speak.

JOJO
(confidentially to Toby)

Hollywood, we gotta stick together cause they are messing with us at all times. I'm sayin hey, you just be bendin over pick somethin' up like a pencil? Whack! Splatt! You get jumped, just like that.

GUIDE

And the sergeant says, "Knock knock." And CottageCheeseAss says, "Who's there?" And the sergeant answers, "we never know!" Next question: Can you dance? Before you get to sandbox heaven we will teach you to move your feet up and down very very fast, which is a form of dancing.

JOJO

Report it? They say you asked for it. This army is this man's army. They only makin' room for us cause they got to.

In SANTA MONICA, Andrew's on his bike.

TERRI
(to herself)

We're the only people we know with a child in the army—a bi-sexual-daughter-foot-soldier.
(a beat)
Maybe if she could be a—a correspondent-soldier. Something embedded. Who do we know in journalism?

In BOOT.

JOJO
(to Toby)

Remember: Private or general, pussy is never what they wanna be alongside, pussy is what they wanna be inside.

GUIDE

If CottageCheeseAss learns to fight but cannot dance, who will celebrate? How will we know we are winning if we can't celebrate? That is a riddle.

JOJO

We gotta get some claws on you Hollywood, you hear me?

GUIDE

Take all precautions. Watch your CottageCheeseAss. Dismissed!

He soft-shoes offstage.

In SANTA MONICA.

TERRI

You raise a kid, all the dangers, always on the lookout—bad friends, bad habits. She gets to be eighteen, she's not anorexic, she's not bipolar or ADD, she's not depressed, she's not alcoholic, she's never OD'd, never been pregnant, she isn't a liar or a cheat, she doesn't steal. You breathe a sigh of relief—just a normal, neurotic, bisexual, half-Jewish achiever!

In BOOT.

TIM
(looking down at his checkbook)
These numbers? They just not doin' the job.

Toby glances at him.

                    JOJO
Hey, I'm not anti-gettin' laid, understand me? I'm pro-that, just on
my own terms.

                    TIM
          (shakes his head, to himself)
Not comin' out right—

                    JOJO
                  (re Tim)
Boy got himself a big ole body, big ole guitar . . .

                    TIM
                 (puzzled)
No sir, no way—

                    JOJO
. . . little bitty skills. Hollywood, you hungry? I'm gettin' the mumbles—

                    TIM
If I can't do the checkbook, how'm I gonna do the income tax?

                    JOJO
                 (to Toby)
Come on, let's go hit the difac, eat up on some army garbage.

       She heads off. Toby looks down at Tim.

                    TIM
I heard the income tax, that's a real sumbitch.

He glances up, sees her staring at him.

> TOBY
> *(extends a hand)*

Take a look?

> *He hesitates, hands her his checkbook. She looks it over, walks after JoJo, beckons him to follow. He rises, trots after them.*
>
> *In SANTA MONICA, Andrew is on the bike.*

> ANDREW
> *(frustrated)*

I can't pull the trigger on this project. Just fly down to Texas and interview this woman who's demonstrating.

> *Terri, reading, glances up at him.*

She's—you know we have a lot in common with her, Terri. She's against the war.

> TERRI

She's a nut-case.

> ANDREW

No, she's totally sincere. She's committed her life to it.

> TERRI

She's camping out. On a road—waiting for the president to drop by for a chat. Please.

ANDREW

It's getting national coverage.

TERRI

It's extreme. And besides, her son is dead.

ANDREW
(amazed)

That's why she's out there. It's driven her there.

TERRI

She's got nothing to lose, Andrew.

He looks at her.

Our daughter is in the army. Do we want to jeopardize her safety by acting out? These people are vindictive. Who knows what Cheney would do, send her on some mission because her parents, movie people no less, are making noise? I mean it. I put nothing past them.
(a beat)
We don't have that much in common with her—that woman. We're against the war, yes, but we're not obsessive about it.

ANDREW

Well, I think we could get involved with her effort somehow.

TERRI
(weary)

Aren't we over-fucking involved, Andrew?

####ANDREW
No. We do nothing! We sit around and—fret. And take pills. And drink.

####TERRI
Do not, do not diss the pill god. She's by my side day and night.

####ANDREW
Positive involvement. It might actually help—both of us.

####TERRI
What are you proposing?

####ANDREW
(hesitates)
I'm not sure yet.

####TERRI
Well, that's a start.

In BOOT.

Easy laughter from JoJo as she and Toby clean their rifles. Tim plays guitar.

####TIM
Well, I jes' mean it's kinda like a friendship.

####JOJO
With your truck. You are friends with your truck.

                        TIM
Well, yeah! Somethin' you depend on, day and night?

                        JOJO
Sounds better than a man, right Hollywood?

Toby keeps working on her rifle.

You stay pissed off at the army you gonna catch acid-reflux.

Toby glances up at her.

                        TIM
                   (watching her work)
Tobe, you better do that over, re-lock.

                        JOJO
"Combat restricted medic." That's what they say you can be. Accept that shit and go for it. Army's got its reasons.

                        TOBY
                   (working on rifle)
I could be as good a combat medic as any guy.

                        JOJO
They don't want women gettin' their butts shot off.

                        TIM
Be a nurse, it's safer.

TOBY

I don't want to be a goddam nurse! And I don't want "restrictions!"

JOJO
(quietly)

They got enough body-parts over there without pickin' up ta-tas and pussies. Makes for bad media. You can still make yourself a medic.

Toby focuses on her rifle.

TIM
(spots a mistake, puts down guitar, takes her rifle, does it expertly)

I can break down, build up any machine you put in my face.

He returns the rifle to Toby, returns to his guitar.

JOJO

But can you fuck it?

Toby can't help smiling.

TIM

JoJo, why you always talk that talk? God's right here, you know. What you need is a hobby. You ever played an instrument, repaired a machine? Things you could fix?

JOJO

I repaired my diaphragm.

TOBY
(with an edge)

Can you fix people?

They look at her.

Can you make people—better? Act better? Be honest? Be kinder? Can you?

TIM

What's she talkin' about?

JOJO

That's why you left college, change the human race?

TOBY

Change people's thinking.

JOJO

Makes you a sucka.

TOBY

Then how they act.

TIM

I don't know about college—

TOBY

It's a progression.

                          JOJO
How people think?

                          TOBY
That's our gift. Democracy. And everybody's entitled to it. Whatever country they live in.

                          TIM
College is tough.

                          JOJO
And how you gonna change people's thinkin' here if you don't speak their language?

                          TOBY
By example. By cooperation.

                          JOJO
In Fallujah? Cooperation in Mosul?

                          TOBY
Once they understand our reasons, our purpose.

                          JOJO
Sounds kinda—lofty to me, Hollywood.

                          TOBY
What we bring them, our democratic spirit. With unlimited conviction, and power.

                         TIM
We just gotta go kill 'em.

            They look at him.

That's why we're over there, isn't it? Before they come over here? Right, Tobe?

            They look at her.

                         TOBY
                       (pause)
You know what I'm thinking now? Transport school. The three of us.

                         JOJO
Transport??

                         TOBY
Rubber meets the road.

                         TIM
Whoa, yeah! I'm good with that. Transport.

                         JOJO
Transport ships right out. They are hungry for Transport. Your scores, you could do Intelligence.

                         TOBY
I got intelligence.

                    TIM
                  (laughs)
Sharp with a checkbook.

                    JOJO
You could keep those Hollywood hands clean.

                    TIM
Tobe's into the grease now. Right, Tobe?

                    TOBY
Into the grease.

> *She rises, leaves them watching her as she crosses to SANTA MONICA.*
>
> *Toby, neat and spiffy in her uniform, stands with her parents.*

                    TOBY
That's what it means, right.

                    TERRI
Transport Specialist—you're a mechanic now?

                    TOBY
I can break down and rebuild a diesel engine, a V-8, practically anything that moves.

ANDREW
(impressed)
No kidding.

TERRI
But why, sweetheart?

TOBY
It's a major support function. Movement and support—how Ops get accomplished.

TERRI
Sweetheart, I'm just trying to understand. We've never had a mechanic in the family. Why would you choose that for a specialty?

TOBY
It's a skill. It's practical, and I'm good at it!

TERRI
Well, I'm not surprised.

ANDREW
(pleased)
The Beemer's been running a little rough lately.

TOBY
I'll take a look.

ANDREW
(amazed)
You never lifted the hood of a car in your life.

TOBY
I know! It's a universe, Dad. I was sure I'd wash out.

TERRI
Out of mechanic school?

TOBY
Mom, it's complex and it's intuitive—computerized—good, dirty, hands-on work.

TERRI
Well, once you set your mind on a task.

ANDREW
Right. Ever since childhood. You know, we checked your options.

TOBY
I got fascinated.

TERRI
On the website.

TOBY
By machinery! Something clicked.

TERRI
I thought Intelligence, for sure.

TOBY
Problems, solutions—exactitude.

(pause, defiant)
I made the right choice.

ANDREW & TERRI
That's what counts.

TERRI
Oh, I almost forgot—I bought scones!

She turns away. Toby exchanges a loving look with her father. He blows her a kiss, and she turns on her heels, strides off.

Kona coffee and maple scones. We're all together, what more could we want?
(turns)
Toby? Toby! Where is she going? Why does she have to wear the uniform in the house? I mean really.
(shrugs)
Okay, half a dozen scones.
(slow dawning—an awful apprehension)
Andrew? Andrew, where is she going?

As they continue to speak, we watch Toby making a trek, moving over and across the various playing levels.

JoJo and Tim fall in beside her and the three of them keep moving, plodding through shifting light.

TERRI
What? No—"overseas" could be anywhere.

ANDREW

She didn't want a scene.

TERRI

No, she's not!

ANDREW

She's going, Terri.

TERRI

Overseas could be anywhere!

ANDREW

She's going.

TERRI
(angry)
No. Andrew, I can't! I can't do it again—every day?? Anxiety, every day? I can't—How am I going to concentrate! On—on scripts and budgets? I can't be twelve years-old again—I run a studio! War-panic and bowel problems? Every day? Every night—bullets, wide awake sweating—combat sounds, screams? Those movies? I need my sleep! I can't go there again. No. My brother? Lose my brother all over again? Relive my awful, fucking adolescence? Bloody bowels? I can't do it. My own kid?

ANDREW

Listen to me. We'll deal with it—we'll—thousands, a hundred thousand families, their soldiers—their, so—children—we'll deal—we'll find a way.

TERRI

No, no she never—oh Andrew, I'm scared! —I'm really really

(pause)

Am I doing this again? My brother Gus all over again? There's no way. I can't do it again. How can I? Can I? Do it again? How? How can I? No—I have to talk to my father. I want to see my daddy!

Toby and her friends suddenly stop moving.

LIGHT bumps way up: the brightest, whitest Light of Arrival. They look around, in shock and awe, and silence.

BLACKOUT

END ACT ONE

ACT TWO

Night. In the dark, distant sounds of gunfire and explosions. Toby sits up in bed in a shaft of cold light, terrified.

A HUGE MAN (on stilts) plastered with U.S. currency strides by. He waves, keeps moving upstage.

From down left a CROUCHING MAN, in a clean, white dishdasha and turban steps towards Toby, making kissing sounds. He approaches and beckons—a large knife flashes in his other hand. He keeps beckoning. She watches him, then turns suddenly hearing VOICES.

A MASKED MAN appears out of the upstage darkness carrying what at first looks like a paint can. As he gets closer we see he's holding a severed head by the hair, and they are arguing, he and the head, in an unintelligible language.

The masked man passes close to Toby and he shakes the head. . . . She SCREAMS. LIGHTS UP on her scream.

The GUIDE, draped in weaponry and his clown pants, is down left, assuming a tough-guy stance.

Toby pulls on her uniform as Tim, JoJo listen.

GUIDE
Yo! Listen up! You are over here now. "Anything suspicious to report, sir?" "Sir, everything is suspicious, sir!" Certify that, and—

"THE MUSTACHE SONG"

Do you see that mustache-driver in the beat-up, pickled van
Five-thousand bristle mustache, black mustache in a van
Well, he loves you! He loves you for
Being here
For bringin' him democracy
Rich home-grown democracy
And he will welcome you with open arms, with wide open arms

And do you see that hiding mustache behind-children-hiding man
Seven-thousand bristle mustache, enemy-without-uniform hiding man
Well he doesn't like you for
Being here
For bringin' him democracy
Rich home-grown democracy
And he will shoot you in the spine soldier, right through your American soldier spine

Look do you spot that rooftop mustache crouching-rooftop- mustache man
Ten-thousand bristle crouching rooftop mustache man
Well he despises you for
Breathing air
And for bringin' him democracy
For rich home-grown democracy
He'll saw your head off soldier, and hold your head up by the hair
Iraqi men wear big black stashes
Count the hairs before the shot
Then separate your friendly Groucho

From your Groucho who is not

SONG ENDS

> *He soft-shoes off stage.*

> *In the TRANSPORTATION SHOP.*

> *SERGEANT TOM, a gruff, burly man, moves around checking everybody's work, talking as he inspects.*

                SGT. TOM
                (calls off)
Drive 'em out! Done and out, done and out!
                (to the group)
I got four Strykers and a Bradley coming in from Haifa Street—dance! Everybody dance!

                TIM
            (to JoJo, low as they work)
How come these Iraqi people don't smile, they see us drivin' by?

                JOJO
              (as she works)
Country all tore to shit. What they got to smile about?

                SGT. TOM
            (to Toby as she works)
Know what I was doin' before I enlisted, soldier? D and C.

TOBY

D and C, Sarge?

SGT. TOM

Damned and corrupt! D and C—I had scraped out the inner lining of goodness, within. Listen to me and learn somethin'!
(to JoJo)
Every bar, every strip joint—whatever I could lay my hands on—beer, weed, whiskey, coke, smack, minor theft, major sex! Nothin' about me was loving. Okay? Why? Because I was teetering, understand? The devil's edge.

JOJO

Okay, Sarge, uh huh.

TIM
(low to Toby)
So they don't like us here, right Tobe?

TOBY

But they need us. That's called a paradox.

SGT. TOM

Self-destruction. And that is no bullshit. Body and soul alike.

TOBY
(to Tim)
We're going to help them and change their minds. That's why we came, why we're here.

SGT. TOM

Judge said, army or jail?

JOJO

So—you enlisted. Right, Sarge?

SGT. TOM

Got in, started screwin' up again. Then one morning I found myself where? In chapel! The chapel, me.

TOBY
(surprised by what she's working on)
Tim, these doors—they're so thin!

SGT. TOM

I believe I was led there. Right to the chapel.

TIM
(to Toby)
Shot up like Swiss cheese holes, bullets popped right through these doors.

SGT. TOM

And this big hand come onto my shoulder. That's how it felt. Held me! Comforted me. Where I am today—a righteous path. I follow it. I encourage you all—get on the righteous path!
(inspecting doors)
What the fuck kinda workmanship is this?

JOJO

Tightenin' up, Sarge.

SGT. TOM
Well, tighten up and get it done.

TOBY
Sarge, these doors here—

SGT. TOM
(to all)
We give good wrench here! We givin' 'em the best. Nothin' leaves my shop, nothin' leaves half-assed, you hearin' me? We hold precious lives in our hands. We gotta be in this clusterfuck of a country because we are doin' God's will! So we do it right.

TOBY
Sarge, about these doors—

SGT. TOM
Oh? Are you informing me? Is this news to me?

JOJO
It's just a panel, Sarge.

TOBY
There's no protection. Paper-thin doors, Sarge.

TIM
Just like them cheapo economy cars, Sarge, like them.

SGT. TOM
It's how they arrived, soft-skin Hummies. Every one of 'em.

                          TOBY

But why would—

                        SGT. TOM

Greatest country in the history of time, and they send us this crap?

                          TIM

Sarge, could we—make a request?

                        SGT. TOM

With IED's like we're takin', on these roads?

                          TOBY

Sarge, I don't understand.

                        SGT. TOM

A request? What request?

                          TIM

Armor plate? Welded plate, Sarge?

                        SGT. TOM

Hey! Since day one. "Being shipped." "En route." "Next container." Blah blah blah, fuck fuck fuck.

                          JO-JO

Any alternatives, Sarge?

SGT. TOM

What's bein' done to us? Buck naked in combat? Bring us here buck naked? It's fuckin' criminal.

TOBY

Gotta be a solution.

SGT. TOM

Solution? Yeah, defensive driving. And kill more rag-head bastards.

TIM

That won't strengthen them doors, Sarge.

SGT. TOM
(looks at them)

Maybe you should go talk to Major Schwanze. Go have a chat. Major loves hearin' from girl soldiers.

In SANTA MONICA.

ANDREW
(looks up from paper)

You see this about the body armor?

TERRI

Did you hear what I said?

ANDREW

They're sending kids on patrol without armor. Trucks, too. I've got to email Toby about this.

                                TERRI
Were you listening to me at all?

                               ANDREW
I wonder—maybe we could do something.

                                TERRI
Am I talking to myself? About what?

                               ANDREW
This. Body armor. Maybe we could inquire.

                                TERRI
Okay, good. Find an address, we'll send money. What?

                               ANDREW
I need to do more than that. I don't know—something—active.

                                TERRI
You do?
                     (hesitates bringing this up)
You know, when my brothers were in Vietnam—Gus was flying and my Dad kept a model of his plane—I hadn't thought about this—the A4-Skyhawk, right in his office hanging on a wire from the ceiling. It moved—when you walked by, or opened the door. He had these maps—South China Sea, all the provinces, south and north. Every morning he read the papers with the maps on his lap and the model plane over his head.

(a beat)

My mother filled notebooks, notebooks full of their letters, Harry's and Gus's, and pictures they sent home. That's all I remember her doing, reading and re-reading their letters, looking at the pictures. Until she went—nuts—

(pause)

And what do we do? Check for her email messages eight, ten times a day? Read every war column, watch every news show. You look at the casualty web site, I know you do! And read the goddam blogs. We try not to wake each other up at four a.m. when we're both lying wide awake—and you think we don't do enough?

ANDREW

I didn't say we don't do enough. I said I need to do more.

TERRI

Where are you going?

ANDREW

Shower and meet you in the bedroom.

(little smile)

Saturday afternoon?

TERRI

(little smile)

How time do fly.

In THE SHOP, Tim and Toby are working.

TIM

I keep tellin' her, but the words don't come out so good.

TOBY

Just be yourself when you call her.

TIM

I can't tell what she really wants me to say.

TOBY

No point guessing. Girls want different things. Just say how you feel.

JoJo and Sgt. Tom head for the shop.

JOJO

Some bad shit is goin' down in there, Sarge. Abu Ghraib, It's not like any regular prison, what I'm hearin'.

SGT. TOM

Hey, Intel needs information, it gets information, however. End of story.
(enters the shop, to Tim and Toby)
You two finish up, grab lunch.

TOBY

Hear you, Sarge.

JOJO
(to Sgt. Tom)
Not only this one here, but Gitmo too, Sarge, I'm hearin'. All kinds of torture and shit—we're doin' it.

TOBY
(overhearing)
What?

SGT. TOM
I'll buy that.

TOBY
No way, Sarge. We wouldn't do those things.

JOJO
We doin' it.

TOBY
That's just rumors.

TIM
So—whatta you want, Tobe? From a guy?

TOBY
What? Well, I know what I don't want.

SGT. TOM
If we treat these bastards like human beings we learn squat. Zero.

TOBY
Come on, Sarge, we don't use torture. That's not who we are.

SGT. TOM
Since 9/11? It's a new ball game, boys and girls.

TOBY
You don't change principles because of a date.

SGT. TOM
And I don't question the Lord's game plan, either.

TOBY
Then it's not a principle anymore, it's a tactic.

JOJO
Sounds like we already did that, Hollywood.

SGT. TOM
Finish up.

TOBY
No, we wouldn't. I don't buy it.

JOJO
Hollywood, this dude's an MP, okay? He works there, he swore to me. He's seen it—what they do to the prisoners.

TOBY
Maybe he's just trying to get your attention.

JOJO
Yeah, well he got some of that last night, too.

Laughter.

TIM
So what don't you want, Tobe? From a guy.

TOBY
(considers)
Anybody who thinks they're "taking care of me," okay? I want someone who knows when to talk and when to shut up and listen. When to let me alone. When to challenge—hug me. Hugs me a lot.
(a beat)
Somebody who makes me laugh, hard. Who surprises me, but—doesn't scare me. Surprises me a lot. Who loves me, just me, totally loves me. But doesn't lose who—he is.
(a pause)
I guess—somebody really really strong, confident, who's also—kind?
(JoJo shoots her a look.)
Yeah, I sound like a wuss.

TIM
Nope. That's who you deserve, Tobe.

TOBY
For instance—my Dad. As an example.
(a beat)
I'm goin' junk yard.

She exits. Tim hesitates, follows her.

SGT. TOM
This whole fuckin' country's a junk yard.

JOJO
Yeah, and it's our junk yard now.

SGT. TOM
God's plan. Right here on the ground. In mysterious ways, before our eyes.

In SANTA MONICA, Terri is on the phone, Andrew on the bike reading a newspaper.

TERRI
(on phone)
No no, she's inside. In the "shop" fixing—carburetors, what do I know? You believe it, my Swarthmore kid!
(proudly)
She's the only one. Of all the people we know. Absolutely, service is a family tradition. Of course we disagree with her politics, but we couldn't be prouder.

In The JUNK YARD. Dusk. Tim and Toby are bent low pulling on a heavy object.

TIM
Gettin' dark, Tobe.

                         TOBY
I'm thinking we can re-do four or five Hummy doors outta this
stuff.

                          TIM
It's gettin' dark. You heard what they said at the gate.

        In SANTA MONICA.

                         TERRI
                     (on the phone)
Her tour ends in September. Then maybe I'll get a night's sleep.
"Tour," you believe it?
                        (listens)
Thanks, dear. Bye. Say prayers!

        The JUNK YARD.

                         TOBY
                       (points)
Let's check that out.

                          TIM
We can't be haulin' this back alone.

                         TOBY
                       (moving)
We'll stack it here, come back in daylight with a pickup.

        SANTA MONICA. Andrew rides and reads.

                    TERRI
                (surprised)

You know, sweetheart, this might sound weird, but I'm starting to sense—jealousy. From our friends. I mean it! I know Toby's always been exceptional, she's always stood out, but this is really unique. Whatever anybody feels about the war—it's an amazing credit. I mean on her resume.

THE JUNK YARD. BULLETS PING off metal...

                    TIM

Tobe, get down!

                    TOBY
                (drops down, rattled)

Tim—

                    TIM
                (takes charge)

Stay down, get lower! Listen to me.

                    TOBY

Where's it coming from?

                    TIM
                (points)

From over there. See that truck? We use that truck for cover.
                (begins to crawl)
You follow me, an' stay down, stay low! Ready? We're outta here—now!

Ground-level low, they scurry off.

In SANTA MONICA. Lights bump up on Andrew and Terri. He dismounts his bike. She's reading a script.

ANDREW
(up energy)

Just don't interrupt me. Can you promise—just, you won't interrupt? I mean I'm spitballing here, but—if it sticks—so.

Terri looks up.

Go ahead, finish your script. You don't have to respond. Just listen.

Terri goes back to reading.

It's only an idea at this point that—appeals in a—it's more personal, as a doc concept. I mean that's what's drawing me to it, but—maybe it's—probably totally impractical. But—
(pauses)
This idea, this film—has, it's never been made.

Terri glances up, then back down to her script.

I know it's never been attempted even.
(little laugh)
Because it's—outrageous! And simple. Basically. At the same time, complex and—and clean. Direct. Impactful.

(deep breath)

Okay. Suppose—if I could, if they permit me—approvals. Quickly. I certainly have the credentials. And I'm certain I could get funding, absolutely, for this? Really fast, without question. It's about the approvals.

Terri looks up, waiting.

Go over there. Follow her. Everywhere. The whole time.
(grins)
I mean it! A father's documentary—of his soldier-daughter. Wherever it goes, wherever she goes. Be there. Whatever I have to do, I'm there, with a crew, or not. Just a camera, depending on—location, etcetera.
(a beat)
Always with her, her outfit. All the moments. The boredom. Anticipation. The action. Fear? The fear. I'm on it. I'm there—I'm right there, with camera.
(watches her)
See what I mean? Simple and—really complex. But rich stuff. And commercial! The "C" word. You love that, right? I mean who wouldn't be drawn to that? It's really—intimate. Not a group of protesters—I haven't discarded that idea, by the way. But it's personal. And -- there's emotion involved, unspoken, but not just observational or political. It's—it's an absolutely unique perspective. Never been done—sensational concept. Probably will go nowhere, right? Never get the approvals?
(a beat)
Is that what you're thinking? Do you want to comment? I mean it is unique. Totally. Go ahead. Please. Am I right?

            TERRI
Andrew—

            ANDREW
Go ahead. I can take it.

            TERRI
       (hesitates, emotional)
You can't protect her.

            ANDREW
What?

            TERRI
This idea. You're not—

            ANDREW
What?

            TERRI
You're not even aware?

            ANDREW
          (realizing)
No. No. Absolutely not. That's not—

            TERRI
Are you?

            ANDREW
Come on. No. That's ridiculous. My motivation? No. I'm—it's not.

(emotional)
That's—that makes me—angry, Terri.

He shakes his head, suddenly overcome. She puts down her script, rises, goes to him, puts her arms around him.

In THE SHOP.

SGT. TOM

Front left door on this Stryker—somebody get on it.

JOJO

Patrol's lovin' us these days, Hollywood. Good doors make friends. Five Unit's sendin' us Hajii juice, half a gallon.

TIM

We still got metal stacked over the yard.

SGT. TOM

Major Schwanze chatted you up yet?

Toby shakes her head, No.

JOJO

There's a surprise, ignoring the grunts.

TIM

All busy with their logistics.

JOJO

Focused on the "big picture."

SGT. TOM
You keep showin' up at HQ somebody's gonna get pissed off.

TOBY
I'm thinking nobody understands jack-shit about this country.

SGT. TOM
Oh yeah? What's the mystery?

TIM
You understand it, Tobe?

SGT. TOM
We hand them democracy on a platter, they shit all over it.

TOBY
Who are "they," Sarge? We don't know these people! We don't even try—Sunni, Shia, their cultures, societies—that should be part of the job. Nobody's doing it, local intel.

SGT. TOM
Is that right? Culture and society?

JOJO
Little kid spit at me yesterday. Whose culture's that?

TIM
They hate us.

TOBY

They don't know us any more than we know them. Why should they trust us?

SGT. TOM

Is that a culture thing to slice off a man's head—on camera? Burn a man, drag his body through the streets, shoot off rifles and cheer? String his corpse from a bridge, howl in triumph like a packa fuckin' wolves? Is that a culture? Or a "society?" If that's a society then it's the society of the devil and I piss on the bible of it!

JOJO

Yeah, I second that emotion.

TOBY

Right.
    (shrugs, rises)
That's what I mean.

SGT. TOM & JOJO

Oh?
Meaning what?

TOBY

Somebody in this army, and I don't mean us, but somebody should know everything about these people—who they are, the city people, the desert people, their history, religion, economy, every hatred, every grudge, every road, every village, what they want, what they need. They don't all need the same things. Local experts. The languages? Instead, we just blow each other up.

And guess what, we're still local-stupid, and we still got shit-for-armor.

> *She exits. Lights remain up in The Shop. She crosses to THE MAJOR'S OFFICE.*

MAJOR
They tell me you've been sitting out there every day, Private.

TOBY
Sir! I appreciate you seeing me, sir.

> *In THE SHOP.*

SGT. TOM
That girl's like a real missionary.

JOJO
Hollywood non-stop.

TIM
Sarge, we need that stacka metal brought back here for the doors.

SGT. TOM
Go grab a pickup, we'll meet you outside.

> *THE MAJOR'S OFFICE.*

MAJOR
Well, I admire perseverance, Private. Apparently this relates to vehicle armor?

TOBY

And individual body armor, sir. Why are we unequipped, sir? All due respect, I don't understand why we're pulling scrap metal to protect our soldiers, sir.

MAJOR
(a beat)

Private, I've been yelling about it since I landed. I'm still yelling. Thanks for your effort.

TOBY

Sir, I'm also wondering about our political approach to the local population. Sir.

MAJOR

Really. Go on, Private.

He looks at her.

TOBY

Sir, is anybody sitting down with local police chiefs, farmers, businessmen, tribal leaders, smoke a cigarette, you know, over tea, break bread and find out what they need? Korans? Bottled water? Cold-weather gear? To win local support? Sir, if we knew specifically what they needed, fighting in their areas, then handed them the supplies, we could show them what would be gained by supporting us. Sir.

MAJOR
(smiles)

We're making great efforts to win them over, Private.

                    TOBY

Sir, all due respect? It's not an effort to get them to like us, but of getting them to accept that supporting us is in their interest. Sir.

                    MAJOR
                (studying her)
Private Rose, what are you doing in Transport?

                    TOBY

Sir, I enjoy the mechanical challenges.
                    (smiles)
Into the grease, sir.

The JUNK YARD, up right.

Toby joins JoJo, Sgt. Tom and Tim hauling metal scrap.

As they cross and come downstage, they pass The Guide in an MP's shirt and red bloomers. He's addressing TWO PRISONERS, heads low, in Muslim dress, and unseen others offstage.

Sgt. Tom keeps going. The others stop to listen.

                    GUIDE

"SONG OF COOPERATION"

Welcome Muslim suspects
Gentlemen suspects be our guests
Enjoy fraternal living secure from night and day

A second home within your homeland
While the outside's kept at bay

We'll learn the customs yours and mine
Hang together all the time
Under water, overhead
You'll enjoy our special chats
Strapped to boards, tied to beds
Our têtes à têtes, our little spats

You can play with snapping dogs here
Dance in women's underwear
(We've got time and time to spare)
So remove those dopey outfits
Wash, don't tear out you ratty hair
Hey, you're forever welcome, suspects don't despair!

SONG ENDS

TIM

Those old boys gonna be dog meat.

TOBY
(stunned)

This can't—this isn't right.

JOJO

Like I was sayin'?

TOBY

We've gotta do something.

                         TIM
Red meat soon. Speak to somebody.

                        JOJO
                     (moving off)
Work on it, Hollywood. Lemme know what you figure out.

> *Sgt. Tom waves for them. Distressed, Toby lingers a moment as the others head off.*

> *In SANTA MONICA, Terri is on the bike with a script, Andrew on the phone.*

                       ANDREW
                     (on phone)
Are you calling me a liar?!
                     (seething)
Yes, I know you're telling me everything you know, you're a "spokesperson," I understand that.
                      (listens)
"It's on the way" is not good enough.
                    (interrupted)
No. No you listen to me. My daughter is on the ground. She says there's not enough armor and they're going to scrap yards collecting scrap metal.
                      (listens)
Do you by any chance have a child over there?
                      (a beat)
Don't "empathize" with me! Do not empathize, just do something. Today. Now. Do it now. Goodbye!

He hangs up. Teri has been watching him. He goes to her, motions her off the bike. She dismounts. He gets on, starts peddling furiously.

We hear the rumble of a distant explosion as light shifts.

In THE SHOP. On a break, Tim strums his guitar, the others sip their coffee. After a moment, Toby enters in a daze, blood spattered.

The others don't notice right away, until they realize she hasn't moved.

JOJO

Yo, Hollywood, 'sup with you?

Toby shakes her head.

TIM
(coming over)

Tobe? What's—there's blood all over you, Tobe. Sarge!

SGT. TOM
(comes over)

What happened? Rose?

TOBY

Not mine.

SGT. TOM
(low, to JoJo)

Clean her off.
(to Toby)

Where were you? Whose blood is this?

TOBY

Passing by.

TIM

Tobe?

JoJo wipes off the blood.

TOBY

They brought them in, I was passing.
(a beat)

A Hummy we hadn't got to yet—with the old doors. These guy—three of them were—bad. I helped move them—with the corpsmen? It—they drove by the market, close by, going through on their way back. Somebody blew the whole market—and the locals. Food they were cooking, food in those big pots? Animals?
(hesitates)

And people—like a big—stew? Toes, fingers, and eyes—bones, ears mixed in with all the animal stuff—bloody stew?
(a beat)

This little hand was inside the Hummy—little child's hand in the driver's lap, and he was all gutted—shaking, shivering, wanted his mama. Blew right through the doors.

(shakes her head)
Blowing each other up. Exploding themselves? Blowing us up? How can—who does that? Where is this?
(a beat)
I forget why. The why's. I forget the why's.
(looks up)
JoJo, when can we go home?

TIM

Three weeks, Tobe.

TOBY

I think—I think we need to be home now.

JOJO

We done. Outta here, Hollywood.

TOBY

That's just us.
(looks at them)
What about everybody else?
(a beat)
I'll get back to work now.

SGT. TOM

You sit down. Sit still.

TOBY

Sarge, I want to get to these doors.

              SGT. TOM
Go lie down, Rose.

              TOBY
           (a rage)
No! I want the doors! We fix the doors, now. The doors!
           (a beat)
I'm—I'm sorry. I need to.

> *LIGHTS fade as she walks away. We hear the slap-pat-pat of a dancing man.*
>
> *LIGHTS up on The Guide, dressed in a doctor's white jacket, a bunch of stethoscopes around his neck. He's got the red clown bloomers on as he dances into the light, finishing with a flourish.*

              GUIDE
Ta Da! See that? Okay, soldier, that's gonna be you. Welcome to Texas and give us eight, ten months, two years, five years, we'll give you feet! Or arms if that's what you need. You got 'em right here, free. Hey, dancin' feet, maybe not light as a feather like me, be a little clunky, know what I'm sayin'? But feets be walkin' again!

"THE DOCTOR'S SONG"
Soldier you're in Texas now
Got yourself a fresh clean start
Walkin' marchin' dancin' feet
Wavin' arms, 'lectric heart
Absolutely

State of the art

So go hug your every loved one
They can visit any time
Nice scummy cafeteria
Cold cock-a-roach buffet
Our always piss-warm coffee
Hey, nothin' spared, okay
Full-tilt recov'ry every day (MORE)

Now you gotta hang tough old buddy
Have patience old budette
It's a time-consuming operation
It just doesn't happen fast
Piecing you back together
Broken-body-building made to last
In rebuilding made to last
Soldier you're in Texas now
Got yourself a fresh clean start
Walkin' marchin' dancin' feet
Wavin' arms, 'lectric heart
Absolutely
State of the art

SONG ENDS

> *LIGHT drops on him.*

> *NIGHT. We hear growling, snarling DOGS. A MAN wearing a silver mask, a woman's bikini underwear and heels, holds wire leashes on invisible dogs.*

A beam of LIGHT catches Toby in underwear kneeling on her bed. The Man moves past Toby, the vicious snapping sounds freeze her rigid.

Two HUGE FEMALE FIGURES (on stilts) move downstage, softly KEENING, covered in blood-red sheets, heads shrouded in black. The red sheets billow as the figures cross and vanish, Toby watching them from her bed.

SLOW FADE TO BLACK.

    END ACT TWO

ACT THREE

SANTA MONICA. Toby, in a pair of boxers and a wife-beater sits in a chair, sucking a can of beer. After a few beats, Terri enters putting on earrings, dressed for an event, hurrying, talking behind her.

TERRI
(calling off)
Andrew, put on the outside lights!

Toby belches. Terri spins around.

TOBY
(smiles)
'Scuse me.

TERRI
Sweetheart, people are on their way—

Toby nods, drinks.

They'll be arriving soon.

TOBY
Okay.

Toby takes a swig, grabs a second can and gets up as Andrew enters, putting on a sports jacket. Toby gives him a finger wave as she passes. Terri gestures to Andrew about her.

      ANDREW

You sleep okay?

  Toby shrugs.

Listen, maybe you forgot, but Mom and I—the fund-raiser's tonight.

  Toby nods.

People are excited that you're home. They prayed for you—I mean the ones who pray.

      TOBY

I appreciate that.

      TERRI

They're expecting to see you, sweetheart.

  Toby winces.

      ANDREW

Just a few words.

  She's not convinced.

      TERRI

A greeting?

ANDREW
(firmly)
A thank you. For their prayers, Tobe.

A reluctant nod, shrug, belch, and Toby exits. They look at one another. Terri's about to get upset.

ANDREW
Just give her a little time.

TERRI
Look at her.

ANDREW
It's entirely authentic.

TERRI
How many days? Has she even washed her hair?

ANDREW
She's doing what she needs to do, Terri.

TERRI
Sleep, drink and belch?

He smiles, shakes his head.

Is it comical? We've got fifty people coming; I don't find it comical.

ANDREW
(calmly)

My guess is she's doing what ninety percent of soldiers do after they get home from war.

TERRI
(flip)

I'll take the other ten percent.

ANDREW
(sudden fury)

You'll take her as she is! Home in one piece! In one piece.

TERRI
(realizes)

I'm sorry! You're right. You're right.

ANDREW
(emotional)

She's home. What's wrong with you? We're lucky! Lucky. We're blessed! She came home.

TERRI

Andrew, please. I know. Forgive me for saying that.

> *He nods. She immediately faces out, addressing her guests.*

Welcome! Welcome, everybody. And thank you for being here. We, Andrew and I—are blessed by the healthy return of our daughter Toby from the war.

(accepts applause)
And we thank you for your love, and for your prayers. We needed every one of you. And now—we're getting some sleep!
(pause)
So. Here we are in the fortunate position of being able to give specific, urgently needed support to our troops in the very tangible form of body armor! Regardless of how you might feel about this war we can all agree that protecting our young people is the primary concern. Andrew will give you specifics—the numbers and cost.
(sees Toby)
Oh. Well, no. Someone else would like a word first. Private First Class Toby Rose.

TOBY
(shaky, a little wave)

Hi.

Toby, in untucked fatigues, not quite up to speed yet, comes Downstage. Smiles.

Thank you. Thank you for—for praying for me. Or just thinking about me. I don't pray, but I accept prayers.
(smiles)
It feels really good to be—home. Thanks!
(turns, changes her mind, gains energy)
So—this fund-raiser, this is an excellent idea. I mean when I got there and—
(shakes her head)
We had to vic stuff from junk yards: refrigerators, old cars, stoves—then weld these panels onto our vehicle doors.

(little grin)

I can weld now. They didn't offer welding at Swarthmore. So—that helped a little. But I never—I tried to get an answer. I mean why were we sent over there, still over there, without enough protection? You know?

(anger)

Our guys got greased—kids are still getting ripped.

(pause)

Somebody—the ones who visit—you know, surprise chopper visits in the blue power suits and ties? They should get down on their knees, apologize to the families of those kids who can't do—regular, normal stuff anymore. It's—I'm still on active duty here and—

(realizes)

It's—I'm ashamed. It's shameful. I mean I'm ashamed—by it.

(a beat)

It's—for me now it's all about the hurt ones. We count 'em up, human statistics, but we never see them—our heroes are all indoors. Their families see them. This major rehab place in Texas, PBS specials? Arms and legs?

(gathers herself)

All I know is the stuff I saw. And who—my bad boys, my buddies I got to be with, work with, fight with, hang with every day, my guys. That privilege. Every day. And—what I'm reading now. I'm reading a lot. And I started to re-think, you know—and—we should get out of there. Now.

(long pause, surprised she said it)

Wow. I actually said that! Anyway, I enlisted—so—I went. My decision. But you know, maybe I wasn't thinking—broadly enough—critically?

> *(shakes her head)*

I can't find a good reason anymore. Okay? Any reason. We don't belong there.

> *(a beat)*

It's really bad. But I still—I'm a patriot! Excuse me. I love my country. Send armor!

> *As Toby turns away we hear SINGING, joyful, up-tempo acapella.*
>
> *LIGHTS Shift to JoJo, Tim and Sgt. Tom upstage left in white army fatigues. They stand close together, finger-snapping, singing, "Keeping Out of Mischief Now."*
>
> *Once through the chorus and the trio gradually begins to sputter. The song breaks down, and red stains seep through their white fatigues. Finally silent, they hang their heads.*
>
> *A masked, muttering, BLACK-SHROUDED FIGURE crosses right to left carrying three heads by the hair. As the Shrouded Figure passes them, the trio follows obediently, offstage, heads lowered.*
>
> *LIGHT finds Toby in bed, panting, in a panic. Terri and Andrew rush into her room, go to her.*

>   TERRI
>   *(embracing her)*

Sweetheart.

ANDREW

We're right here, Tobe. You're with us.

TERRI & ANDREW
(simultaneously)

You're home. You're here.

She lets them comfort her. Her breathing eases.

TERRI

Just a bad dream, sweetheart.

TOBY

I need to get dressed.

Confirming something for herself, Toby rises, begins to put on her full uniform.

ANDREW

Tobe?

TERRI

How about a nice shower?

ANDREW

What are you doing, Tobe? It's five a.m.

TOBY

I'm—in a hurry.

                    TERRI & ANDREW
                    (simultaneously)
A hurry for what?
Why the uniform?

    They look at one another.

                         TOBY
To tell people. Okay?

                         TERRI
Tell who, what?

                         TOBY
In uniform. Before I get out.

                        ANDREW
Tell them . . . ?

                         TOBY
Now. That we're making a mistake.

                        ANDREW
A mistake about—the war?

                         TOBY
                       (nods)
In uniform. This war. Staying there is a mistake.

    Andrew and Terri look at one another.

TERRI

Well, we heard you, I mean this is wonderful, but—

TOBY

It's not wonderful!

TERRI

No, sweetheart.

TOBY

Nothing is wonderful. I have to. I know I have to. But it's not wonderful.

TERRI

I'm sorry.

ANDREW

Tobe—can't you be disciplined for that? Speaking out?

TOBY

In uniform.

TERRI

But why now?

ANDREW

When you—how did you decide this, Tobe?

TERRI

What's the difference?

(to Toby)
Why not wait till after you're discharged, sweetheart?

TOBY
(looks at her)
Who would I be if I waited?

A pause.

ANDREW
So. Wow. Okay, let's find out what your rights are, in uniform, legal rights. You're a citizen. I'll get on line, or maybe I should call Jack.
(notices her)
Terri?

TOBY
I'm sorry, Mom.

TERRI
(rattled)
You're a person of such conviction, Toby—it scares me.

TOBY
You are, too.

TERRI
(shakes her head)
My convictions are selfish.

ANDREW

Look, Tobe, where do you start? You can't be the only soldier thinking like this.

TOBY

I'm not.
(squares-up her cap)
But who's saying it?

ANDREW

Do you want help?

TOBY

Help?

ANDREW

Your rights. To speak out. Information.

TOBY
(looks at him)
Maybe I could use some help.

LIGHTS SHIFT. Andrew and Toby zigzag from level to level as Terri is all showbiz on the phone.

TERRI
(on phone)
I want you to get another writer on this; I think he's tapped out. I know, I know he brought you the project, I respect that. Fire him. Get a fresh pair of eyes, somebody hungry, maybe uncorrupted. Well, just—hunt. You'll find one. Then put your tushies together

and squeeze out a good, firm second act! No you can't come in, I'm working at home. Gotta go. Love you too, bye.

(a new call)

Hello, who's this?

LIGHTS up on Andrew and Toby making their circuitous way to SANTA MONICA while Terri stays on the phone.

TOBY

It won't work, Dad! I can't stand up alone on some random street corner in uniform and make speeches. I'll look like a lunatic.

ANDREW

He said you could still participate in demonstrations.

TOBY

In civvies! Demonstrating in civvies won't make the point. So why were they all smiling at me in that office? What was that about?

ANDREW

I didn't notice.

TOBY

It's like they'd never seen a soldier in uniform before.

ANDREW

You could still voice what you think, express what you feel about the army, in civvies.

                    TOBY
                (looks at him)
I love the army. The military didn't start this.

                    ANDREW
I understand that.

                    TOBY
So why can't you make that distinction?

                    ANDREW
It was a slip of the tongue.

                    TOBY
Just knee-jerk, anti-military sixties bullshit.

                    ANDREW
No. A learned response. "Just following orders?" We've seen what that can lead to. I'm sorry, the military isn't some victim in all this—it's—an accomplice.

> *He keeps walking; she hesitates. Troubled, a strange uneasiness passes through her.*

In SANTA MONICA.

                    TERRI
                (on phone)
Yes, who is this?

> *Andrew and Toby arrive home.*

ANDREW

Terri, we're back!

TERRI
(on phone)

Hold on, please, she just walked in.
(low, to Toby)
For you, some army thing.

TOBY
(low)

Did you remember the scones?

Terri nods, smiles, points to them.

(on phone)

Hello?

LIGHTS shift to a podium, down left. The Guide, dressed in a belted safari jacket, hair in place, wire-rim glasses, strides to the podium. Below the waist he's wearing small, tight wrestling shorts, black dress shoes, and black socks.

GUIDE
(hands on podium, silent)

Does anybody speak the language? There will be no questions unless you speak the language, and wrestle! If you satisfy that profile, write, or rather jot your question on a three-by-five card, submit it now, and begin to stretch over there on that mat.

"MR. SECRETARY'S SONG"

Dear my fellow patriots
Fine women, brave young men
Let me say it is
Delightful!
Oh, such an uplift
To touch down amongst you once again

Your ever-constant valor
Recent triumphs, huge success
(all kept secret from the press)
Have won you honors, due respect
A nation's heart-felt best
Plus, one small, well-earned request

Stay!
Your orders are to
Stay on
Brave women fine young men
Extend your tour your duty (what a tour!) and
Stay
Stay on

For serial bravery
Only just beyond the call
Stay on to make a difference
 Seal the deal, we'll have a ball
Fulfill the promise made together
When we saw the statue fall

God bless you all and
Stay!

Stay on
Brave women brave young men
God bless me too and
Stay!
Stay on
Stay on
Stay on

SONG ENDS

> *Light shifts to SANTA MONICA.*

> *Andrew and Terri pace, in turmoil. Toby stands stock-still. Terri and Andrew make a beeline for the bike. He steps back, lets her get on. She begins peddling furiously. He paces again. A silence.*

ANDREW
(half to himself)

I will not be a coffee-table radical about this. I swear it!

TERRI
(peddling)

A what? He won't be a what?

> *He continues to pace.*

ANDREW
(stops pacing)

What about Canada?

                    TERRI
              (stops peddling)
What? Canada!

                    ANDREW
                  (to Toby)
You could go to Canada—speak out from up there.

                    TERRI
Yes! Yes, Vancouver! It's not far at all.

                    ANDREW
Does that—solve it? I think that might solve it.

                    TERRI
It's a very cosmopolitan city.

                    ANDREW
You could start a blog. I love this, Tobe.

                    TERRI
From a really nice apartment. Remember the Kellmans? You'll stay with them first. I'll call.

       She starts peddling again, fast.

                    ANDREW
Listen—we are unique military parents: a major studio executive and an academy nominee. What's that group called? The lawyer told us.

TOBY

MFSO. Military Families Speak Out.

ANDREW

We'll join. Condemn the war, get press, start shouting, factual shouting, become ultra-visible, while you're doing it up in Vancouver.

TOBY
(flat)

Gettin' rad, Dad.

ANDREW

We—we'll march. Take to the streets—all over the country. Meet other military families, start new chapters.

TOBY

Outrageous.

ANDREW

Totally immerse ourselves.

TERRI
(gets off bike)

Andrew.

ANDREW

What?

TERRI

You might have to totally immerse yourself. I have a job to think about.

ANDREW

You'll take a leave. You can take a leave.

TERRI

I'd get fired.

ANDREW

A soldier's mother? Never.

TERRI

For "other" reasons. Corporate reasons.

ANDREW

They wouldn't dare.

TERRI

They're tight-ass killer-cunts in suits. I'll be finished.

TOBY

You know—nobody really listens to deserters.

They look at her.

ANDREW & TERRI

What?

TOBY

When I don't answer the callback. I'd be a deserter if I went to Canada.

They look at each other.

ANDREW

You create a network up there, you organize a—a global resistance network! You'll be a new voice, a brave new voice.

TERRI

We'll fly up every weekend. Alternate weekends.

TOBY
(decisively)

I can't.

(pause)

I can't run. Besides, it gets really cold, my feet—I hate cold weather.

A silence.

ANDREW

So—sweetheart, what's that leave us?

TOBY

Refusing an order to report? Court martial. Jail.

TERRI

Jail?

ANDREW
You won't be heard in jail.

TOBY
I won't, right.

ANDREW
But if that's your choice.

TERRI
Andrew, for chrissake.

TOBY
The stockade.

TERRI
Oh god, my agita—

TOBY
Incommunicado maybe.

ANDREW
Toby, nobody will keep us from seeing you.

TOBY
(struggling)
I know my buds—are packing to go back.

TERRI
Stop.

TOBY

I'm guessing everybody'll go back.

ANDREW & TERRI

That's immaterial.
It's their decision.

TOBY
(little smile)
Bitching a whole bunch about it.

ANDREW & TERRI

You've got a mind of your own.
We'll find a way.

TOBY

It's only a four-month tour. That's it. Four more months.

ANDREW

You're on a mission, Toby; you've got an agenda now.

TERRI & ANDREW

You can't go back.
It's out of the question.

TOBY

Four months? That's what they said on the phone.

TERRI

They're liars! Remember?

TOBY

And the lawyer said I could even start a blog over there. They can't keep me from writing.

TERRI

Listen to me! We'll—Dad and I will do anything.

TOBY

You know, I'm here now, I watch TV, go online, the radio, walk around, visit the mall. It isn't—it's totally unconnected to the war here, what we're doing over there? It's just an afterthought.

TERRI

I mean it. We're all in this together.

TOBY

I'm in uniform like some—curiosity. People stare! I'm like an L.A. alien.

TERRI

I'll—I'll quit the studio. There, I said it! I'll quit.

TOBY

And no one cares. I mean the "home-front" doesn't exist! It's not here.

TERRI

And we'll have enough money once we sell the house—even in this market, and—leave. Just leave the country.

TOBY

Everybody's—shopping. Or talking about *American Idol*.

TERRI

Oh god, listen to me. I feel liberated already. Andrew, do you believe what I'm saying? Do you believe me!

TOBY

We're at war and nobody's involved with what's going down. Nobody's fucking obsessed.

ANDREW

We are fucking obsessed.

TOBY

I mean you are, yes, of course our families are.

TERRI

We can move anywhere. The three of us together! Anywhere we want.

TOBY

But the country's not in the war. It's just us. The military. It's only us.

TERRI

Pick a country. There's a whole world we can choose from. A house on a lake, or—in the mountains! A little village in—somewhere with cheese! Or wine? Someplace welcoming. A country totally hospitable to Americans—what's left, Uruguay?

A silence.

       TOBY
       (finally)

I made a commitment.

       TERRI

No! You were a child then.

       ANDREW

Tobe, you gave the army what they asked for.

       TOBY

Not about the army.

       TERRI

You were there. You served.

       TOBY
      (shakes her head)

Or politics.

       ANDREW

Your first commitment is to yourself, Tobe.

       TOBY
       (relieved)

Second.

       (smiles)

I'm second. My joes first.

She turns away, puts her cap on, squares it up, and in SHIFTING LIGHT, starts traveling.

LIGHT stays up on Terri and Andrew.

Toby is joined one at a time by JoJo and Tim along the way. As they meet up, they link arms, keep moving...

TERRI
(building panic)
Andrew, when she was born, bringing her home, the station wagon, remember? From the hospital, "How will I protect her?" I was terrified. Ever since—that's what—all the time—even when I'm not aware of it—at work, in a meeting, on a set, there was this—worrying, this tick tick list: "What time is it? Where is she now? Is she okay? Is she safe? Is she almost home? Okay. Okay. She's safe." All the time, all the time, "How can I keep my kid safe?" And then she enlists in the fucking army!
(a beat)
A girl? Having a girl, girl-worry, the physical fears—awful abused awful battered rape-crap, rape—but not war, never war. That's for mothers of the boys. It's a trade-off, rape-worry us, war-worry them. I've been dealing with rape terror, but not war terror. It's not my area!
(pause)
Then she's home. Here. Her own bed. And I tiptoe, watch her, hear her breathe. And—I can sleep again! So now what? Am I supposed to flip a switch? She's-back-in-a-combat-zone switch? How do I—what do I do? Reprogram myself? What do I do now? These feelings—the need doesn't dry up, to protect her. It gets—it's even worse! Out of my hands again, out of control, totally out of

my goddam control. Ineffectual. Helpless! Oh, right, I can send armor! Or protest. Terrific.

(a beat)

She is unsafe again, Andrew! Big-time danger, constant danger—and—without me. And I should what—let go, right? Let it go and say, "The army's taking care of her. It's the army's job again." The army? They can't even equip her properly! Because it's—they're not doing their job, which unless I'm mistaken, is war!

(a pause)

She's a girl, Andrew, she's not supposed to be there. That wasn't the deal. I didn't sign up for this. I can't—I'm fucking helpless. My kid's back in danger, she's twenty, and I'm still stuck with this—ridiculous—this—this yearning, this "make her safe"—with fucking prayer.

The three friends, arm in arm, pass The Guide. He's parade-marching fatuously, wearing his red bloomers and spiffy field jacket, carrying a rifle, as they move offstage.

A spurt of GUNFIRE. The Guide ducks, looks around . . . stillness. A blaze of LIGHT. EXPLOSION. BLACKOUT.

LIGHTS UP on The GUIDE crumpled on the ground as a huge, tan Humvee car rolls across stage left to right.

It stops, opens, and Toby steps out, staying low, cautiously followed by Tim and Jojo. They quickly gather up The Guide.

Hugging the ground, and hustle him to the open car door, close it behind them as LIGHTS DROP and the car rolls off right.

LIGHTS UP bright.

The Guide stands downstage in an over-large hospital gown, cap, boots, head bandaged, arms behind his back.

SONG: "STATE OF THE ART"

GUIDE

Soldier you're in Texas now
Got yourself a fresh clean start
Walkin' marchin' dancin' feet
Wavin' arms, 'lectric heart
Absolutely
State of the art

So go hug your every loved one
They can visit any time
Nice scummy cafeteria
Cold cock-a-roach buffet
Our always piss-warm coffee
Hey, nothin' spared, okay
Full-tilt recov'ry every day

Now you gotta hang tough old buddy
Have patience old budette
It's a time-consuming operation
It just doesn't happen fast

Piecing you back together
Broken-body-building made to last
In rebuilding made to last

Soldier you're in Texas now
Got yourself a fresh clean start
Walkin' marchin' dancin' feet
Wavin' arms, 'lectric heart

> *His right arm comes around: it's a shiny prosthetic, rising slowly into a salute*

Absolutely
State of the art

SONG ENDS

> *Holding in salute, the hand of the prosthetic pops off the wrist, dangles. He holds the salute, looking at the hand without moving.*

LIGHTS FADE OUT SLOWLY.

THE END

To the Memory of Four Men of the Theatre:

>Jacques Levy
>
>Al Carmines
>
>Ken Howard
>
>Tony Roberts

Their wonderful theatrical imaginations enriched my playwriting, and their profound friendships continue to enrich me.

Acknowledgments

TO KATE, ABOVE ALL. And for their enthusiasm and help along the way, my special thanks (in no special order) to:

Nancy Mette
Frank Coppola
Richard Liebman-Smith
Keira Naughton
Jim Naughton
Michael Posnick
Lonnie Carter
Robert Montgomery
Kevin Graham
Robert Gold
Paul Bresnick
Dana Wallace
Barbara Strong
Jay Strong
and my worthy editor/publisher Karl Weber

David Epstein

About the Author

DAVID EPSTEIN'S PLAYS have been produced Off-Broadway, at regional theatres across the country, and abroad. He wrote the screenplay for the film *Palookaville*, which began life at the Sundance Festival, was honored at the Venice Film Festival, and opened in the United States and worldwide to critical acclaim. Mr. Epstein has written screenplays for the major movie studios, and his films have aired frequently on network TV and on PBS.

Mr. Epstein has taught at Colgate University, at NYU, and at Yale. He is a graduate of The Yale School of Drama. He lives with his wife Kate on eastern Long Island and Oahu, Hawaii.

MORE PLAYS BY
DAVID EPSTEIN

In three plays (***Exact Change, Hair of the Dog,*** and ***Shades***), Epstein brilliantly sketches the bleak, despairing—and howlingly funny—underside of contemporary American life. "Fizzes with talent"—Benedict Nightingale, *The Times of London*

ISBN 978-1-953943-80-4 • $22.95

A series of three plays—***Mahalo, Desperados,*** and ***Arky***—tracing the story of an American family navigating a years-long crisis driven by a child's mental illness. By turns harrowing, wildly comic, and deeply affecting, ***The Arky Trilogy*** vividly captures the shocking twists of life as experienced by one family.

ISBN 978-1-953943-35-4 • $22.95

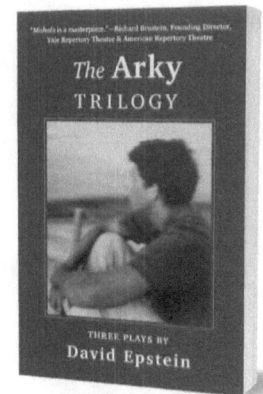

AVAILABLE WHEREVER BOOKS ARE SOLD
For a special price on the three-volume David Epstein collection, visit www.rivertownsbooks.com

www.ingramcontent.com/pod-product-compliance
Lightning Source LLC
LaVergne TN
LVHW091623070526
838199LV00044B/907